Praise for Randi Zinn and the *Beyond Mom* community

"Randi provides an important voice and support system for women looking to maintain their unique identities 'beyond mom.' I have always been very impressed by the depth and thoughtfulness she brings to every part of her own life. And as a fitness professional, I am especially impressed by her commitment to health and wellness as one of the central pillars of her work. All mothers need more people like Randi in their lives!"

—Mahri Relin, founder & creator of Body Conceptions fitness

"This book will provide a unique opportunity for all mothers to benefit from the wisdom and honesty of a thoughtfully cultivated community of dynamic and inspirational women. *Beyond Mom* is not about leaning in or out or left or right, it is about discovering your own path through and beyond motherhood."

—Naomi Schoenkin, founder of Six Degrees of Mom

"Randi Zinn knows communities. She's adept at forging connections between moms at a vulnerable and transitional state. When we become moms, there's no handbook, we have to rely on our girlfriends and communities to get us through the rough spots. . . . As a woman who wants to be defined as more than just a mom, while also relishing my delicious family life, I'm so glad Randi's there to celebrate and enumerate the possibilities. This is a book for me and all the other mom entrepreneurs who are incubating ideas."

—Nicole Feliciano, author of *Mom Boss*; founder and CEO of MomTrends and TheShoppingMama.com

"Becoming a mom doesn't mean we relinquish the desire to stay connected to ourselves, our careers and to other women—Randi gets that. Through the creation of *Beyond Mom*, Randi sends the message that women not only deserve but *need* opportunities to develop ideas, nurture mind and body, and maximize our potential. Randi is not only inspirational in the way she lives her own life, but in her desire to motivate and encourage other women who want to go 'beyond' being a mom to live with intention and purpose. Randi is a leader and a teacher. . . . Her skills are invaluable to any woman looking to redefine her role in life after motherhood."

—Rachel A. Cedar, MSW, founder of You Plus 2 Parenting

"Randi has bucked all assumptions and become even more of a force of nature since becoming a mom! She is the only person who can get me up at 6 a.m. on a Sunday to exercise with a bunch of other equally bleary-eyed mothers because I (and they) know that at her events, we will meet amazing people who make us feel a part of something bigger than ourselves. Because of the community she has built, I feel empowered as a woman, a momma, and an entrepreneur."

—Ali Smith, photographer and award-winning author of *Momma Love: How the Mother Half Lives*

"For years, Randi Zinn has been thoughtfully building an exciting and inspired community of women who have decided that while motherhood is central to their lives, it does not define them. The *Beyond Mom* community inspires rich conversations about the meaning of motherhood, work, and womanhood in the twenty-first century."
   —Natalia Mehlman Petrezela, assistant professor of history at The New School

"Randi has brilliantly created a resource for what all working mothers know: You can't do it alone! She has brought together an amazing community of moms with experts to guide them on the journey to wholeness and success. I wish I could have experienced this when my son was growing up."
   —Barbara Biziou, author of *The Joy of Family Rituals*

"Randi is a powerful force for what life as a mother and woman is all about. Her movement, *Beyond Mom*, is one that invites women to lead as mothers from their strength as women. As a coach and strategist for women, my work in teaching the principles of fierce and feminine resilience and leadership is emulated by Randi's work with her community of moms. It is clear that today, our children, the next generation, need for their mothers to be happy, healthy, and whole as women so that they can serve as the kind of role models they need. Randi, through *Beyond Mom*, is able to serve, support, and inspire women to take responsibility for nurturing themselves as they step more fully into the role of mothers. She is walking her talk and paving the way for the women she serves."
   —Laura W. Campbell, women's transition strategist, relationship and divorce expert and coach

"It's easy to think that being a mom requires you to be that and only that. Moms have interests, passions, businesses . . . lives. The concept of *Beyond Mom* exemplifies that and Randi is the ultimate connector for these moms."
   —Kaity Velez, cofounder of Well-Rounded NY

"Randi's quality of truth struck me as not only refreshingly honest, but vital. I have witnessed her blossom and build a community of women that look to her as a leader and an innovator. She leads by example and serves as the foundation of what it means to push past traditional stereotypes and lead a *Beyond Mom* lifestyle."
   —Jasmine Takanikos, JTCG Consulting

Going Beyond Mom

HOW TO ACTIVATE YOUR MIND, BODY & BUSINESS AFTER BABY

RANDI ZINN

Foreword by Melinda Blau

Skyhorse Publishing

Skyhorse Publishing books may be purchased in bulk at special discounts for sales promotion, corporate gifts, fund-raising, or educational purposes. Special editions can also be created to specifications. For details, contact the Special Sales Department, Skyhorse Publishing, 307 West 36th Street, 11th Floor, New York, NY 10018 or info@skyhorsepublishing.com.

Skyhorse® and Skyhorse Publishing® are registered trademarks of Skyhorse Publishing, Inc.®, a Delaware corporation.

Visit our website at www.skyhorsepublishing.com.

10 9 8 7 6 5 4 3 2 1

Library of Congress Cataloging-in-Publication Data is available on file.

Cover design by Jenny Zemanek

Print ISBN: 978-1-5107-2400-6
Ebook ISBN: 978-1-5107-2402-0

Printed in the United States of America

For my parents, who saw my gifts
long before I did.
For my husband, who urged me to step
into those gifts.
And for my children . . . when you were
born, so too was the woman I was
meant to become.

Contents

Foreword
by Melinda Blau

I STARTED PAYING ATTENTION TO MOTHERS when I became one myself in 1969. As a journalist, I began to cover motherhood and the many relationships it involves—with children, partners, parents, siblings. And this, among other things, is what I've learned: As challenging as being a mother was in the seventies, it is even more so today. I wish there weren't a need for *Beyond Mom*, but there is.

I began studying (and worrying about) this current crop of moms when my daughter became a mother, and I a grandmother. We were both, as Jen spontaneously put it one day, "in the Motherhood Union."

I had never been as close to my mother as Jen and I were. We had the same taste in clothes, music, and movies. We also enjoyed similar activities, like yoga and tennis. And in 2002, when we launched our website MotherU.com, and began talking to other mother/daughter duos, we realized we weren't alone—women in their 30s and 60s were more alike than different, a phenomenon we described as "generation overlap." Jen and I never wrote "our" book—she raised three sons and I pursued other writing projects. We also suspected thirteen years ago that it was too early in our motherhood and grandmotherhood careers to write about them. How right we were!

One thing I didn't see coming was the inordinate and unfair pressure mothers now bear. In this way, my generation of mothers were not like our daughters. Sure, it had always been a daunting task to raise a child, and we had our share of maternal angst as we flooded into the workplace. But motherhood nowadays, in varying degrees, has become a preoccupation. To be a mother is to be all things to your child and, worst of all, to hold yourself responsible for how a child turns out.

Mothers today need a life raft, and Randi Zinn is throwing them one. Swimming in the turbulent seas herself, she has identified the greatest challenge of motherhood: to retain and nurture a strong sense of self. *Beyond Mom* encourages women to be more than one role—to be there for your child and also for yourself. It gives mothers a place to air their doubts and share their experiences. It gives them permission, and resources.

Tons of research confirms that it's healthy to step into different roles. By all means, be Mom and be proud of it. But you can also choose to be Healthy Woman, Yogini, Entrepreneur, Hard Body, Sculptor, Musician, Volunteer—you name it! You'll be happier and healthier for it, and so will your children.

Randi Zinn walks the walk. She doesn't just tell mothers to take care of themselves. She protects her own stamina by exercising and eating right and taking downtime. She doesn't just give advice about being an entrepreneur. She is a savvy businesswoman and generous collaborator. And she doesn't just share strategies for juggling roles. She takes on the challenge herself of wearing many hats and living a passionate, energetic life—without feeling guilty.

Most important, Randi doesn't just preach "community." She is building one. Her many talents notwithstanding, she is a connector. She reaches out to like-minded souls and welcomes them to share their experiences and wisdom.

And now she's capturing it all in this book, which is filled with her own smart ideas about going beyond—hopefully, redefining—motherhood, as well as the best strategies she's learned from others. It will confirm, inform, and embolden you to be yourself, whether you're just starting the journey or are already entrenched in the struggle.

—Melinda Blau, author of *Family Whispering*
and the bestselling *Secrets of Baby Whisperer* series

"What does *Beyond Mom* mean for me? I think it means being fully rooted in the reality that I am a mother and my kid is my favorite person on earth. He's just this amazing person I get to hang out with. He's not the only person I get to hang out with. There are other people I love supporting, there's other people I love hanging out with, and I'm very clear that as much as he is totally in love with me and loves to hang out with mom, that's going to change, and that's going to be hard for me. It's only going to be harder for me if I don't have my own life. *Beyond Mom* means continuing to have my own interests and my own passions outside of motherhood that support me financially and spiritually and emotionally, so that I can be a good mom and support myself when he's no longer tugging at my apron strings fifty times a day."

—Alexandra Jamieson, mother, author of *Women, Food, And Desire*, co-creator of Super Size Me, and host of Her Rules Radio

Introduction

Being a psychotherapist for almost two decades, I've witnessed many young mothers feel guilty about having needs and desires outside of their role as a mom. Since being a mother is a singular aspect of the self, it is impossible for that role to fulfill all the other aspects of a whole human. All women had lives, dreams, and desires before having a family, which don't disappear once that family materializes. Prior to becoming a mother, you may have been a creative career person, a friend, a lover, a writer, a seeker, a thinker, and more. Those essential aspects of self, regardless of how developed they were, still need your time, attention, and consideration in order for you to be fulfilled. Prioritizing some level of self-care and self-consideration also spares your children the pressure of being your sole source of happiness (since they can only fail). Too much self-sacrifice in the name of motherhood will also inevitably create resentment, which can lead to the Martyr Mom Syndrome.

—Terri Cole, licensed psychotherapist, relationship expert, and founder of The Real Love Revolution

WELCOME TO THE JOURNEY OF MOTHERHOOD! I realized as my own pregnancy unfolded and my son arrived, that the journey wasn't just about learning how to take care of a little person, but was also about embracing the person that *I* was becoming. I started to see the world differently and I unexpectedly experienced an evolving confidence in my own abilities and ideas as each month ticked by. But what really blew me away was that my entrepreneurial spirit was also born with my son.

Then, to my even greater surprise, I found out I wasn't the only one. On the playground, I met moms who had left their corporate jobs and were launching businesses during their children's naptime, writing books, building websites, going back to school, opening restaurants, you name it. Why was it that I had assumed new motherhood meant slowing down and losing momentum? I was discovering the opposite—an undefined, unnamed, unstoppable creative force that bubbled up around me. I also recognized through too many conversations with lost and confused new moms that the current work force does not leave room for the mom who wants some flexibility and support as she discovers both her mom self and the mode to be productive. No wonder so many women are discovering a new, entrepreneurial way.

And with these two realizations, my own creative juices began to turn, and before I knew it, *I* was building a business while my son was napping. And *Beyond Mom* was born.

But as quickly as I identified these surprising realities, I also identified ways these driven women were being underserved:

❶ These powerhouses lacked a community! How could that be? With thousands of mommy groups, baby play gyms, and one-stop-shops for everything a mommy could want, how did these idea-driven women not have a way to support, connect, and discuss with one another?

❷ These same women, the ones with the seven-figure *a-Ha!* ideas, and numerous kids, and endless amounts of fire to get it all done, often lacked the tools to take care of *themselves*. At the end of the day, these same women were having difficulty carving out time to exercise, get a haircut, read a book, or take a break. Self-care is a big issue.

While New York City seems to be brimming over with this intriguing population of high-achieving women, I also recognize that there are far more women who feel these same soul-stirrings but likely have no idea how to begin. Or even if beginning is okay. These stories of women "doing it" are not perfect ones—we all struggle to find balance. I don't want to make you feel, dear Mama reader, that you are so behind on your life. What I will share is that I have learned quite a bit from these manifesting mamas, and I now believe there is a formula to taking your idea by the horns and your spirit by the hand. I have tested out many of these concepts as I've created my own business while facing the realities of motherhood. Let's be honest, as women we may experience a burning desire to grow our ideas, but once we have children it can be difficult to summon our motivation and/or find the support to step forward.

Does this conundrum sound familiar?

Are you suffering, swimming in your own desire to grow, but unsure and unclear of where to begin?

Does it sometimes feel that you're damned if you do and damned if you don't? Damned if you take time away from your kids, but damned if you don't heed your calling?

Is there a balance to be struck?

I don't claim to have all the answers, but I do know a lot of women who know one thing for sure: *The more connected you are to your self, the better woman you are overall.*

May I state an obvious and often forgotten fact? Too often we forget that we must be well-rounded and centered *individuals* in order to be grounded and present mothers. The more connected to the woman you are, the more able you'll be to show up as the mom. Some assume *Beyond Mom* means we somehow forget our mom self as we cultivate our entrepreneurial self. It is the opposite, my friends. The more self-connected we are, the more we'll be able to be great moms. Even if we've taken four hours for a run, a development call, and the writing of our business plan, the hours we have with our kids before bedtime will be so much more fulfilling. Why? Because when a deep part of ourselves is satisfied, we are like a vehicle that has been fueled. Suddenly we have more energy to give to others.

I've created this book for those of you who feel the longing to create something of your own, but don't know where to start. I've taken the lessons I've learned as a woman navigating this shaky dynamic, and also as a woman who listens to hundreds of other women a month in my workshops, and I have culled tangible and actionable insight. I've included a community of advice from some of the most fantastic experts I have access to, and real life stories from some of my favorite *Beyond Moms*, providing you with a multitude of perspectives, tidbits, and support in the areas I think you need it most. I hope that as you read forward, you hear a choir of voices sharing what they know to be true, lovingly guiding you as you figure out your unique formula for success. These are the people that have created my reality of support and empowerment, and I'm honored to share them with you.

If you find yourself simultaneously rocking the stroller while combing the self-help section at Barnes and Nobles wondering *what's next for me?*, you've arrived in the right space, the right hub of encouragement and insight. Let me help you find the forest through the trees. Getting back into the groove

"*Beyond Moms* are doing this fascinating thing. They are in this culturally and historically unique way, trying to balance person-hood and motherhood. We never had to do that before. A mother wasn't a cultural role so much before as it is now. You became a mother, raised kids, and you ran the farm, or gathered, or hunted with nets, or whatever it was that you did. Now, we've separated motherhood, person-hood, and work. The women I'm describing are finding unique, important ways to link them all back together again."
—**Wednesday Martin, mother, anthropologist, and author of *The Primates of Park Avenue***

of your life might be difficult, but it is not impossible, and some of it is more basic than you would imagine. I hope everything you're about to read will make you feel incredibly hopeful and driven.

Whether you're in New York City, Chicago, or Dallas, the *Beyond Mom* Community is alive and well—and we welcome you. None of us have it all figured out, but we're all navigating the same questions so just know that by picking up this book you're beginning a very important process: the development of the person who holds it all together, the woman inside the mother.

Welcome to your journey!

What is *Beyond Mom?*

Throughout this book, I'll be referring to the *Beyond Mom* Community and to the work I do. I'll be explaining how I've shaped a brand and taken something I'm passionate about and putting it out into the world. But on a daily basis? *Beyond Mom* is a vehicle to share content and connection meant to empower and inform women at this critical time in their lives (entering motherhood, establishing a new identity, and figuring out what's next for themselves, personally and professionally). We offer daily content on our website www.beyondmom.com written by many experts in their fields, as well as experts on the nuances of this phase of life (so in many respects, experts on just walking the walk). Our most popular content is the beloved *Beyond Mom* interviews, the real life, honest truth behind some incredibly driven moms who are also building their dreams. We also have interviews with experts as well as our popular podcast, On Air with Beyond Mom, available on iTunes and Stitcher. What I think we're best known for and loved for are our in-person events, held mostly in New York City, but I foresee that growing. We gather women for meaningful conversations, potent networking, but most importantly, we aim to invigorate women by reminding them of their own depth and the depth of others. Several times a year, I also host a day-long yoga and self-care retreat for moms at my Hudson Valley home and studio. These days remind me how needed these moments of pause are, as well as how much we can support one another if we slow down and open up. Periodically, I coach women who are on the *Beyond Mom* path, guiding them on the steps for better self-care and work productivity. I love those in-depth, in-person conversations. They reveal so much.

What I want to share most with you and *Beyond Mom* is that it's a work in progress. It's not fully evolved, perfectly baked, or making a zillion dollars yet—but I'm putting it out there anyway. As you read this book, I want you to know that I'm not further ahead, necessarily, I'm also figuring out my next steps, my business model, the way in which I can both work and be present for my kids. I'm in the trenches right with you. I hope you can take the information I offer you not as the information from someone who has it perfect or has reached the ultimate goal (because none of that is true), but from someone who is very passionate about what she does and who is simply brave enough to put it out there, even if it's not perfect yet. Does perfect even exist? I've decided *no*, it doesn't. But you, my readers, are seeking right along with me, so let's share together.

"Motherhood, the most important, beautiful, awe-inspiring, and exhilarating thing known to woman, is only a fraction of what I do. I'm also a certified personal trainer, a TV gal, radio host, author, I manage my website, I'm helping build fitness software for Microsoft, I sit on the advisory board of health apps . . . all of that is what makes me a *Beyond Mom*."

—**Jenna Wolfe, mother, TV journalist, fitness expert, and personal trainer**

Does this truth-telling make you feel more comfortable going forward? I hope so. I want this journey to be one that is enjoyable and relatable for you, one in which the person sharing with you (me) feels like chatting with your bestie on the couch, right next to you. And that's exactly how I see myself and *Beyond Mom*.

This Book has Been Guided By . . .

Hundreds of conversations with the *Beyond Mom* Community, and thousands of my own moments. I've pinpointed the most important tips and guidance to integrate into your life in ways that are approachable and practical. These concepts make the difference between an anxiety-ridden existence and one that is grounded, peaceful, and full of joy. I've started with the premise that we must ground ourselves first in our body, then our mind, and also in relation to the community around us—I argue it's the only way to launch anything into the world, particularly a business idea that emanates from the evolving new you. This book will guide you to getting back to your best, most steady self, and from there, how to embrace and launch what your soul is ready to share with the world. This shift can be life-altering; it has been for me.

> "Sometimes just being a mom is enough, and makes you beyond. Taking that 'beyond' further is when there is fluidity and an ease when confronting various challenging moments throughout the day."
> —**Debra Ross, mother, acupuncturist, and herbalist**

Who Am I?

My *Beyond Mom* story started way before I even thought of becoming a parent and frankly, it was a pretty rocky time in my life. On October 19, 2005, only a few days past my twenty-fifth birthday, my father was killed in a plane crash. Life after that day felt daunting, painful, and mystifying. He was my best friend, and I couldn't imagine moving forward in my life without him. In retrospect, it was this devastating event that launched me into womanhood. My father was a visionary entrepreneur, having invented some of the first solar technologies in the 70s and developed a variety of energy-related companies. I was now in charge of the fate of these companies. He also owned a general aviation airport in my hometown. Yes, I lost my father in a plane crash and now had to think about running an airport.

I was twenty-five years old, living in New York City, trying to make it in the media industry. The entire picture of businesses, employees, wills, and taxes, seemed impossible for me to handle. But, like so many experiences in motherhood, I had no choice. I figured things out because I had to. And I found the right people to advise me because giving up was not an option.

Of course, one day I woke up and realized while I had metaphorically landed the plane, I was so far from the light-hearted, creative woman I had been before I lost my father. I also had this buzzing sensation in my spirit telling me that the heartbreak I had been through was going to allow me to deeply connect with and help many, many people. I read a quote that said, "When your heart breaks open, God floods in." I started to understand this statement on a deep level because to me, God is love, and I started to feel the need to give more love to people around me. I could honestly feel their pain and felt capable of supporting them through conversations, hugs, and even stillness. I started practicing yoga to heal my wounded heart and get back inside my body. I made powerful discoveries during that time about myself, about the universality of loss, and the possibilities of healing. I decided to become a yoga teacher to bring balance in my life between the physical and the spiritual, between being of service and managing my father's business legacy in the way he would have wanted.

Fast-forward to 2011—my husband and I got pregnant. I had no idea what the events of my life would amount to, let alone how

I would find a balance between motherhood and my other passions. But I felt a stirring in my soul, a light in the midst of all the sadness, the pain, and the struggle to navigate uncharted territory. Somehow, everything I had gone through had offered me an opportunity to dig deep, to connect with myself and with others through their struggles, a universal language to support people navigating change and longing for more. I wasn't sure exactly where to start, but I had contacted a *feeling* inside of myself that said, *share your story, your passions . . . and you will help people.*

Before my son was born, I designed and launched the very first version of my website and allowed myself to write what I was passionate about. I didn't have a particular goal, I merely wanted to write and see what evolved. My perspective seemed to stick with readers. When my son was born, my own stirrings seemed to knock a little louder. Some moments, I admit, I wanted to run from it. *I don't have time to build a business right now!* But the more I spoke with the women I met at the playground and at baby classes, the more I felt my confidence developing. *My unique story, my personal talents, the losses I have suffered and navigated, created my personal ability to create something special, something only I can share with the world. I have to do it.*

I felt my Dad cheering me on. Nothing ever stopped him and nothing would stop me.

PART I

Discovering the New You

"*Beyond Mom* really resonated for me because when I first became a mother, I didn't know what my identity was going to be. Was I just going to be a mom? Was it going to be split between being a mom and being in the workforce? I realized there's a way you are everything—you can be everything all rolled into one. For me, it's being a mother and being able to be a role model for my daughter and for other children out there to show that you can do a lot more."

—Jenny Powers, mother, founder of Running With Heels, podcast host of BroadCast: Broads Building Businesses

CHAPTER 1

The Body

Why is the Body Where We're Starting This Conversation?

IT WOULD SEEM UNNATURAL NOT TO start this entire conversation where it all begins: our bodies. Our body is the vehicle for the nascent experiences of motherhood—the journey begins with our ability to conceive, carry, and birth another human being.

Of course, we have many members of the *Beyond Mom* community who have adopted, and twenty-four hours into round-the-clock feedings, they are just as physically drained and euphoric and hormonal as the rest of us. But in this section, my focus is on the childbirth connection.

Some women love being pregnant, are in touch with the miracle of it, and swoon over the power of bringing life forward. Others of us (myself included) found the physical process of pregnancy and birth to be a very mixed bag—some parts incredible, and other parts a real challenge, particularly to my identity. Let's face it, once you become pregnant, your body is no longer your own. We are often run by cravings, exhaustion, and possibly nausea. If, like me, you experienced a miscarriage, the early portion of pregnancy can be anxiety-ridden and you might have found yourself moving more gingerly and cautiously. The welcomed second trimester often brings with it an alleviation of symptoms and worry, but then we watch and feel our bodies change. Let me describe some of the things that happened to me, and maybe some of you will relate. My nipples became shockingly huge and dark, my thighs and bottom widened. As my belly began to swell, I noticed my skin changing and itching. As I gained weight, my joints ached and I moved slower. I'll never forget the night I woke up with a muscle cramp in my calf—let's just say it rivaled labor pains! I remember struggling to find clothing I liked and made me feel pretty, and most difficult for me was being told that I had to be on *rest* during many junctures of my pregnancy. Avoiding activity, and even prolonged periods of walking, really messed with my mind.

Now let's jump to what happens when the baby is born. Most of us leave the hospital completely in love with our new baby and immediately know that whatever we went through to bring him or her into the world was 100 percent worth it. But reality quickly sets in, and we realize we have a long haul in front of us. We are bleeding like we've never bled before (why did no one ever tell me about that?), we are stitched *somewhere* and it isn't comfortable, our breasts are huge and when milk comes in, it's *painful* (why didn't anyone ever tell me that either?), our nipples get ripped apart by nursing for the first time, and our bodies are oddly misshapen from having lost a large amount of weight in approximately one day. And there's still more on there. Oh, and sleep. Not so much of that happening.

Do I sound like I'm complaining? What I'm trying to do is spell out the very basics of what childbirth does to our bodies (and this is the no-major-complications list), and why it can feel extremely challenging to find our physical strength (and motivation) again. Even when we have gotten through the initial few months of healing and perhaps returned to our work or daily schedule, we notice that things aren't quite the same, physically or mentally.

Over many conversations with hundreds of women, I have realized that many disengage from their physical bodies in order not to deal with it. They tell themselves that they don't have time, or that their bodies hurt too much, or that they can't bear to leave their children (or their husband with their children). But what happens, whether in a few months or a few years, is a sense of *blah* that begins to infect other parts of a woman's life. There arises a lack of confidence in one's own strength, sexiness, and overall capabilities. The women who come to me for coaching are angry with themselves for letting it all go, but they did so because on a daily basis, it seemed easier. My heart breaks for these mamas because I feel their conflict. I'm not saying it's easy. But I do believe it's possible for everyone to get back to their physical body, regardless of the help they have or don't have with their children, or with the amount of money in the bank. It's also possible to reconnect with your body even if heavy duty, intense exercise isn't your thing at this point. What I'm addressing is a shift in mindset and a commitment to want to feel better in our own skin. Let me go deeper on why this choice is such an integral one.

The Lens of Limitation

One of my favorite teachers, Patricia Moreno, founder of the IntenSati method and mama of three, says that we prepare our bodies to face the rest of our lives. Have you had to haul your child up a flight of stairs when they're having a tantrum? I don't think I need to give any more examples as to why our strength allows us to be competent parents. We can lift, transport, and deal with our kids (and all their equipment) when we have developed our bodily strength. But it goes deeper than that.

Many people walk through the world wearing a "lens of limitation." *I'm not strong enough for that, I'm too small to lift that, I'm not educated enough to write that, I'm too weak to take that class.* We go through life telling ourselves what we are not capable of and all the reasons why not. As humans, we tend to need tangible proof that something is possible—it's why scientists will spend lifetimes proving a theory—we need to see, to know for sure. As women, we are no different. What are we truly capable of? The only way to know is to *do*.

But first we have to find a way in, and that means removing our lens of limitation. Let's first and foremost commit to change our language. *I can do that. I'm willing to try; I have so much to say so I'm going to write it.* Language changes toward the positive are huge motivators. When we remove the lens of limitation we begin to see possibilities, and quickly step forward, toward our future rather than hovering in our dissatisfied present. When we make it through that spin class, lift that heavy weight, or at the very least *show up* to something we've been intending to do, just as Patricia says, we become more prepared for whatever else our day has in store for us. Suddenly lifting the baby, rushing down the street, or dealing with that stressful phone call feels more manageable on every level. We are being conditioned to be better-functioning human beings. And it begins by shifting away from a lens of limitation and toward a lens of possibility. The proof is in the pudding.

How We Carry Ourselves Is How We Sell Ourselves

You can always spot a person who feels strong in their body. They sit taller, they walk with confidence, and they tend to complain a little less. Why? Because they are grounded in their body and, therefore, in their mind. I want to confirm here that I'm not interested in a person's weight or how intense a workout you can withstand. I'm talking about strength and determination. Strength can be found in a yoga class, a Pilates session, a hike through the woods, or a stroller walk with a community of women. Determination is possible regardless of what size pants you wear. The mindset I'm describing comes from feeling that you run your physical self, and not the opposite. This connection with our body occurs when we find ways to move that feel approachable and enjoyable.

Studies show that how we carry ourselves immediately effects how others perceive us. If we are eventually going to speak about embracing our entrepreneurial ideas and running with them, we must carry ourselves with strength and confidence. When we meet people for the first time (inherent to networking and taking meetings) we're immediately perceived through our physicality. If we are getting back into the work force and interviewing, we are judged by the way we hold space in the room. We hope we are moving past a world where women are judged professionally by their weight or appearance. I know women of many shapes and sizes that carry themselves with confidence and grace. They all know how to move and command their presence and it shows in the way they carry their body. These women are taken very seriously. With personal strength comes confidence and poise.

Isn't this how we want to present ourselves to the world?

Physical Pain

Many women come to me for guidance because their postpartum lives have been marked by a lot of, or even just low-grade, pain. It makes them more tired than they should be, less patient than they want to be, and makes all their *Beyond Mom* dreams seem unattainable, when they're anything but!

Movement has always been my medicine. I've understood that when I don't move, I become plagued by aches, pains, and odd and inexplicable injuries. For many of us after pregnancy, we lose our core strength, stemming from a weak pelvic floor and the strain of carrying a baby. Fact: if our core is weak, so is our back. A weak back equals pain. And pain clouds our perception and turns our thoughts toward the negative.

Movement, however we can find it, keeps us limber, our blood moving, our lymph clearing, and, hopefully, makes our core stronger. Just like they say a healthy gut effects our entire immune system, a strong core affects the quality of our movement and whether we experience our body through discomfort or through freedom.

I'm going to share a little more of my story, and I hope it helps you understand that the route to movement and body strength isn't always a straight one. I've spent the majority of my life as a dancer, a yogi, and then a fitness enthusiast. I'm what many professionals refer to as hyper-flexible. When I was young, I would do moves which, after a few drinks at a party, garnered a few laughs, some wows, and let's face it, some male attention (yes, I was that girl in my twenties). But the body can only handle so much, and after two pregnancies and vaginal births, followed by the carrying and nursing of my babies, I began to experience, for the first time in my life, pain. Pain in my left hip, shoulder, and neck. Pain that made the aftermath of my workouts unbearable because I was making the mistake of ignoring the discomfort so I wouldn't miss the movement that makes me feel so happy for so many other reasons. Finally, I hit a wall and I began to think about how I wanted the rest of my life to look, how I wanted my body to feel, how I wanted to carry myself. Did I want to be in pain all the time? Did I want my movement to be unsafe because I was unstable? No, most certainly not, and I began to see that this would effect how I carried myself, my business, and my ideas, into the world. Since this realization, I've taken a break from my intense workouts and replaced that time with seeing a physical therapist. I've learned so much about how my body has been operating by working with her. She has given me exercises that I do each day (sometimes on the floor with my baby, or after the kids are asleep). I'm dreaming of a time when there's no more discomfort and my movements actually feel fabulous. When I stand tall without tightness. In this case, slowing down movement for a goal that will eventually bring me more empowerment and confidence is an excellent choice, and I would encourage any woman and mother to do the same.

Personal Confidence

I've learned a lot from having to slow down my body in pregnancy and during this time when I have to shift my movement toward physical therapy exercises and away from the classes I enjoy so much. I've learned the beginning of the sacrifices of motherhood—that it isn't always about you anymore, and you have to know when to shift gears toward selflessness.

I look back and I'm grateful for these lessons. I also learned that movement and physical strength are very important parts of my personal confidence, and I have met hundreds of women since starting this community who feel the same; they work to find their path in making those important connections.

I've also learned that I must take care of my body for anything else to work well for my family.

Let's get back to the idea that if we are not in pain but merely telling ourselves that working out is not for us, perhaps there is another way. I always defined myself as a dancer/yogi type. I didn't overly involve myself in fitness crazes—I didn't need more than I had, or so I thought. When the baby weight hung on and I felt the itch to get my blood flowing, I knew I needed something else. Nervous and completely lacking in confidence, I took my first spin class. It was one of the hardest things I'd done in a very long time (if not ever). In moments, I shed a few tears, mostly because it was hard to believe I was actually doing it. But when I got off that bike, I was elated. Never in my life did I think I was able to make it through a spin class—I just didn't think I was made that way! I left feeling invigorated, inspired, and, you guessed it, extremely confident. If I could do this, what else was I capable of? Again, we are training our body for all other aspects of our life.

People ask me all the time how I do it. How do I work out to the level I do? How do I make time for it? How do I tune in so keenly to what my body needs, whether it's movement or therapy? In my mind, I have no other choice! I simply must care for my body, not only to make sure I'm painfree, but to know what I'm personally capable of. After a tough workout, you can be certain that I'm ready for that meeting with a complete stranger who can help build my business. That I stand with confidence taking photos at my *Beyond Mom* events. Even after my physical therapy sessions, I feel aligned and stronger, knowing that I'm steering my body toward a space I want to live in. Again, it's not about confidence in my *appearance*, although that does, of course, improve with exercise, it's about confidence that I can forge ahead, and handle whatever comes my way. Best of all, I know I'm strong enough to grow my dreams.

Let's Assess

Have I convinced you to get moving, to tune into the state your body lives in, to assess whether you're in need of support to get where you want to be, or are you ready to take the movement plunge? I hope so. There are so many reasons that go deeper than just our physical well-being. But before you jump in, we have to make sure that some very important questions have been asked and answered to avoid injury and tailor the endeavor to you exactly. After all, I want you to be successful!

How Was Your Fitness before Getting Pregnant?

You've decided you're ready to move. Even if you had to slow down during your pregnancy, your fitness level prior to pregnancy is very important. The body has distinct muscle memory, so even if it's been a year, or more, your body remembers certain movements and retains levels of strength. If you've never been a fitness person, take this into account as you begin. Do you want to consider working with a trainer to be sure you are doing things properly? Should you start a beginner yoga class to be certain you understand the alignment? Part of confidence and safety is starting at the appropriate level.

How Was Your Pregnancy?

There are a plethora of complications that can occur during pregnancy and some may require intervention, or delay you getting back to your workout. Some issues may not require anything more specific than modifying your workout. As an example, many women experience Diastasis Recti, which is the separation of the left and right abdominal muscles during pregnancy. Working out is not an issue, but certain abdominal exercises can worsen the condition. Be sure to consult your physician to understand what actually happened during your pregnancy so you can adjust your physical recovery accordingly.

How Was Your Delivery?

The wild card! We never know how our delivery will be or what parts of our body will be affected. Though I felt ready to work out, my back was really hurting from nursing and holding my son, and the stitches I had in my perineum took longer than anticipated to heal. With my daughter, because my birth was furiously fast, there was less stress on my body from pushing for a long period, but I still had to contend with stitches. By the second time around, I knew I had to invest in a highly supportive sports bra when easing back in. The early days of working out postbirth are accompanied by large, heavy, sensitive breasts. This requires extra support from your sports bra. Investing in one helped me feel ready even though I was physically in a different phase. Pay attention to the realities of your birth experience, as they will inform how you ease back into your physical repertoire.

Did You Have a C-Section?

It's so important to remember that a C-section is major abdominal surgery. Every layer of muscle is cut, so please make sure to take that into consideration when you start getting your strength back. Seek out DVDs or instructors in your area who specialize in working with women post C-section. Discuss what to avoid and what to try when you have your follow-up appointment with your OB-GYN.

How Is Your Nutrition?

After giving birth to my first child, it felt like I had no time to cook for myself. I felt exhausted and depleted and struggled to produce enough milk. I realized quickly that I needed more nutritional support. Postpartum, we really do need an increase in protein and vitamin-rich foods to support our own healing and the nourishment of our babies. When we begin working out, our needs only increase. We need energy to support our output.

I understand the impulse to diet. Our bodies are carrying loose skin and ten pounds of extra water for the first three months. But I prefer to encourage the women I speak with simply to be mindful, eat healthy foods of many colors, and to avoid too many simple carbohydrates. We don't need more pressure mentally. We simply need some healthy lifestyle tips to live by. And we most certainly need our nutritional fuel as women getting ready to develop who we are and launch who we're becoming! For more on this, read one of my favorite books for inspiration on healthy living as a pregnant and new mama: *Mama Glow* by Latham Thomas.

How Is Your Energy?

Let's face it: motherhood is exhausting. So I don't expect you to answer this question with an affirmative, *Fantastic! I feel like I'm fifteen years old—let's do this!* I ask the question so you can realistically choose your activities and get the help you need, if you need it. Perhaps if your energy level is really low, you start with yoga as opposed to spinning, just to see how the movement feels. Maybe hiking outside and breathing fresh air feels like the best way to move. Perhaps you get your hormone levels checked to be certain whether you need some assistance (acupuncture has been a huge asset to me with my hormonal concerns). Your vitamin levels may also be low (Vitamin D, Vitamin B, and iron can be big culprits) and perhaps you need to add some extra supplements to help with your sense of vitality. The main point is to be clear as to where you really are, and respond accordingly. If you're simply tired from broken sleep, well, I feel you, sister. But working out will also help get through that. Those endorphins are miracle hormones.

Let's Get Moving

You've bought yourself some new active wear, gathered some gym class pamphlets, and cleared some time in your schedule. Now what? It's time for a chat with yourself, particularly that voice telling you how out of shape you are and there's no way you can make it through a class or a jog.

What Do You Enjoy Doing?

After there's been so much focus on the new bundle in your life, it can be hard to answer this question. Sleeping may be a logical answer at this time, but I'm asking you to think about what you enjoy *doing*—do you enjoy being around a lot of people? Do you prefer doing things solo? Do you like to dance with your girlfriends? Do you enjoy skiing? Ice skating? Bike riding? Do you love the outdoors, or do you prefer indoor activities? Do you like going to the ballet? Are you fascinated by Arnold Schwarzenegger and Jane Fonda? These questions might sound silly, but they actually inform the kind of individual you are and what kind of workouts might best suit you. Depending on how you answer these questions I might send you to a yoga practice, a dance class, or a weekly hike with your neighborhood mom-friends.

What Did You Like to Do as a Kid?

The answer to this question can inform so much. If you're having trouble defining what you, in fact, will or won't enjoy in a new workout, remember what you loved as a child! Were you the quintessential cart wheeler? Were you on the swim team in high school? Did you love competitive color war at summer camp? Yoga was logical to me when I moved to New York City at twenty-one because I had been a modern dancer in college. It felt good in my body and kept my mind peaceful as I navigated busy city life for the first time. But post-baby, I needed to lose the weight. I had rarely, if ever, been to a fitness class. Frankly, the gym bored me. So what did I love as a kid? I loved dance, I loved to bike ride, and I loved upbeat, rhythmic music. It's no wonder I now take spin class and cardio dance at least once a week.

In my mid-thirties, I enjoy pushing myself past my perceived boundaries and seeing what I'm capable of. I'm also confident enough in myself that if it isn't my best performance, so be it. I'll also add that in today's day and age, there are so many fun hybrid workouts fit for almost any kind of person, and a million ways to access them. Get creative with your own ideas and believe me, something exists out there for you to try.

Be Willing to Experiment

So often I hear women say, "I went to try a class at this new Pilates studio near my house today. The instructor stunk and her music was horrible. Forget it, I'm done." This attitude, unfortunately, will get you nowhere fast. Like anything, all are not created equal and beauty is in the eye of the beholder. When you begin this process you must give patience to the process of finding what you love. If the first Pilates class sucked (according to you), try a different instructor. If Pilates isn't working for you, try a sculpting class. If boot camp was too high-impact, try spinning. If the class setting makes you feel embarrassed, try some fitness DVDs and get your sweat on in your living room. If you're longing for fresh air, take walks with your baby or hike in the woods near your house. Get my drift? You must put yourself out there and stay open-minded. Have fun with it and try new things. Keep your eye on the ultimate goal: you want to develop your strength, body, and mind, to approach your life with positivity and a can-do attitude. It has to start here.

Be Forgiving

I admit, this is a tough one. Back to the beginning of this whole spiel: our bodies have been through a bit of a war scene. We feel wobbly and achy, and like we're not our own. And now I'm telling you to go and shake it with confidence. It's tough. But trust me, if you show up again and again, in less time than you think, you will find yourself more confident than you believed possible. Your body will begin to respond to the challenge and you will feel your confidence rising.

In the midst of those awkward early days, the only thing you can be is *forgiving* . . . and *kind*. You must remind yourself that it takes *time*. It's not going to feel great immediately. You're stepping through that door because you have a bigger picture in mind. Simply love yourself for being brave enough to show up.

Suggestions for the Mama with No Village

Today's parenting culture is a far cry from the days of "it takes a village." Many of us (myself included) do not live even a car ride away from our immediate family. Having inadequate support in the way nature intended can feel like the biggest limitation of all. How do we find the time required to strengthen our body? Do not fear, here are a few suggestions I have, based on scenarios I've witnessed for many of the women in my community:

1. If you cannot afford daily childcare, can you find the budget for a college student who might be interested in making a few extra dollars, a few hours a week? Can you utilize that specific time for your workout and self-care? If you can find the few dollars, I argue it's money will spent.

2. Do you have a friend in your neighborhood who might be willing to babysit swap with you? I know of friends who take turns watching each other's kids while the other goes to work out. And believe me, the one who stays at home with the kids gets a workout too. No cost, and everyone wins.

The incredible amount of live streaming, on-demand, DVD workouts that exist are mind-boggling. You can pretty much have anything right in your living room. Workouts can happen while children nap, or even with your children. A dear friend of mine did Pilates videos with her two little girls at her feet while she stayed at home with them. When they were small, they'd simply lay around and play. As they got bigger, they started to join in! I love a woman who teaches her daughters physical fitness!

❹ If you're comfortable with it, many gyms and YMCAs have childcare. If that even sounds like an option, go in and check it out. See if you could imagine leaving your child there for an hour while you get your sweat on. This option could be very economical and conceivably fun for everyone.

Some of us can afford a nanny and more regular help. Some of us have husbands that fully support our needs for self-care and bodily strength. Some of us even have grandmas and grandpas nearby. And still we make excuses. In this case, we simply need to get out of our own way. We must remind ourselves again of the kind of life we truly want to live. Some women I know actually feel *guilty* for hiring a babysitter and using that time to workout. *Whoa, sister.* Is there anything more important than our own health and well-being? Do we really think we can carry the world on our shoulders and not put fuel into the vehicle that hauls the whole load? I think not. Can we shift our perspective and recognize that there is no better investment we can make than in our own selves? Embracing this as fact is step one to becoming the woman I believe we all want to be—strong, empowered, and prepared to unleash all of her potential.

Making Time for Your Workout, by Mimi Benz, founder of Sweat Shoppe Spin Studio

"Making time for your workout is the biggest challenge. Even owning a fitness business, I have that challenge! I find myself sometimes going three or four days without being able to work out. And that frustrates me more than anything. I own a fitness business and I can't work out? I think creating a schedule and just sticking with it is the solution. Don't make excuses! My daughter woke up every three to four hours one night. I got maybe three or four hours of broken sleep. So naturally, I didn't really want to work out. Just do it. If you let that kind of stuff get in the way, more and more things are going to come up, so just create a schedule for yourself and stick to it as best as you can."

Insights on reconnecting with your body through movement, by fitness expert and founder of IntenSati method, Patricia Moreno

"I remember after having my baby and having been so physical previously, that when going back to the gym, all I could do was cry, cry, and cry. I couldn't help it. I cried so much because after all those years of investing in my physical body, I was back at zero. I was back, but I couldn't even hold a plank or do one sit-up, or do anything I could do before with my core. It was a really scary time. What I realized was the body is so capable of miracles, as those of us that have given birth know quite well, that it's also capable of repairing itself and restoring itself better than ever before.

"What gets in the way of that ability of the body to restore and renew itself and to be stronger than before, is the stress and the worry. One of the things we can always do that can help us tune back into our strength, even when our body doesn't feel the way it used to, is to move any way. Anytime that we move, whether it's a walk, whether it's putting on some music and just feeling the energy of moving itself.

Movement has energy, and movement brings health.

Movement also helps you shift your lens and your filter, and it helps your body restore itself to balance. I'm not even talking about big workouts, I'm talking about standing up and stretching, feeling the expansion of your body by reaching the arms out, to the more vigorous exercising that we can do once our body is healed.

"Really making it a priority is what I want my message to be, that movement is not a luxury. It's something we need to invest in on a daily basis if we really want to have the quality of life most of us yearn for because, quite simply, the body needs movement.

"Write a list of all the benefits you know exercise has, not just for you—we're not just talking about your waistline and getting your flat abs back, we're talking about the benefit it is to your children, to your partner, to your work, to your sanity. When you start to see the investment in movement and in reconnecting to yourself and filling yourself up with that strength and vitality and peace of mind, you see how it radically improves your ability to handle the stress—and there's nothing more stressful than trying to fit all these things in amongst crying babies. You will be able to handle all these things more efficiently, with more grace, more strength, and you'll do it in a way that you're proud of."

"*Beyond Mom*, to me, celebrates the feminine archetype of motherhood as an expansive role. It's not about being a super-mom or striving to be perfect. It's about wholeness—knowing how to find center even on those days when you feel completely off track. A *Beyond Mom* optimizes her unique gifts in order to nurture the welfare of her child. In order to do this, she must know herself. I am a *Beyond Mom* because of my deep commitment to cultivating self-awareness. I have always been inspired to explore and contemplate topics like humanity, evolution, healing, and the role that spirit and nature play in the dance of life. While that sounds lofty and intangible, it's also very practical because it inspires insight and has a direct impact on everything that I do. As the creator of the Anya Method and founder of Studio Anya, I weave together the sacred and the mundane as part of my approach to Mind & Body Fitness."

—Courtney Bauer,
mother and founder of Studio Anya

CHAPTER 2

Your Mind on Motherhood

LET'S GO ONE STEP FURTHER. WE began with a serious discussion about our bodies and got real with ourselves. Now let's discuss our mental state. Let's just state the obvious: if we paid attention to the media and to the photos of our friends' Facebook feeds, we'd assume that motherhood is pure joy and everyone is feeling completely and emotionally fulfilled. Raise your hand if you actually feel this way (I hear crickets). Motherhood is *amazing* and *inspiring* in so many ways, but the early days can be *tough*. And even now, as a mother of a five-year-old and a one-year-old, it's still tough. There are so many reasons why motherhood can be a challenge to our minds: some are quite technical and scientific. Others are the result of how we are designing the flow of our lives around our children. Either way, our mental state is beyond worthy of a chapter in this book. Without our mind, we can go no further on our mission. So, let's dive in with the most important question . . .

What Shape Is Your Mind In?

The mental state for women in the first year after giving birth can vary from profound highs to crippling lows, and everything you can think of in between. The highs can occur during cuddly moments with our babies, victorious moments when we finally get the car seat/stroller/Pack 'n Play to bend to our will, and moments of firsts (smiles, laughs, and steps). But daily? We are often exhausted, malnourished, and perplexed by the abrupt changes in our life. All of this is dissected in the section below. But my first suggestion before we dig in is to ask yourself, and write down in a notebook, how you would define your mental state. Do you feel confused? Mentally dazed? Do you feel resentful of your child or partner? Do you feel like your emotions change from moment to moment, hour to hour? In other words, emotional swings? Does missing your old life leaving you feeling antsy and dissatisfied? Do you feel guilty for having so many "negative" emotions when the world says you're supposed to be blissful? First of all, let's drop the *shoulds*—they help no one. Can you accept that motherhood is hard and you are normal to have this mélange of feelings? Your body is not the only thing affected. Your mind is also on this journey of change and transformation. And change, my friends, is almost never easy.

Once you have addressed what you actually feel without judgment, you can actually begin a dialogue based on some facts. Let's begin with the biggie.

Postpartum Depression

Or the "baby blues" as they're also called. According to studies, Postpartum depression can begin any time during the first two months after you give birth. Symptoms may include:

- Irritability or hypersensitivity
- Difficulty concentrating

- Anxiety and worry
- Crying or tearfulness
- Anger
- Negative feelings such as sadness, hopelessness, helplessness, or guilt
- Loss of interest in activities you usually enjoy
- Difficulty sleeping (especially returning to sleep)
- Fatigue or exhaustion
- Changes in appetite or eating habits
- Headaches, stomachaches, muscle or backaches

Some women with PPD believe they can't adequately care for their baby or may harm their baby. Experts agree there's no single cause, but rather a combination of hormonal, biochemical, environmental, psychological, and genetic factors. Current research indicates that one of the strongest predictors of PPD is depression or anxiety during pregnancy.

Many women need help navigating this difficult time, whether through psychological counseling or the use of anti-depressants. There is no wrong way. The only right thing is to be honest and get the help you need so you can find a happier space in your life.

Though I was lucky to have only what I would call "average" bouts of tears in the weeks following childbirth, many women I know navigated this very difficult experience.

How Is Your Sleep?

Sleep. The long lost lover of parenthood. I don't care who you are, how much money you have, how much family you have around you—you will never sleep as you did when you were single and sans bébé. There are those strange anomalies of children that start sleeping through the night at about three months of age, and those moms seem oddly composed and a wee bit smug. But most of us cannot relate to this version of things. Our perception becomes bleary and broken and we find ourselves forgetting our thoughts mid sentence.

Insights on Postpartum Depression and support, by perinatal clinical psychologist and assistant professor Elizabeth A. Werner

"While pregnancy and giving birth can be an exciting time for you and your family, it can also be a time of great stress and a huge identity transition. The experience may bring up issues from your past; relationship problems with members of your family may be intensified. Combine these issues with the dramatic hormonal changes, body transformation, and lifestyle adjustments of the perinatal period, and it is no surprise that depression is the most common complication of childbearing. In the first few weeks after childbirth, most women experience what are called the 'baby blues,' and feel overwhelmed, sad, tearful, and/or anxious. Having these sorts of feelings during a time that many feel 'should' be purely happy can be surprising to many women, and some may feel guilty and distressed. Typically, the symptoms of the baby blues remit after a few weeks. However, for some these symptoms do not go away and can become more severe. Postpartum Depression affects more than twenty percent of all women who have given birth. Women with PPD may experience depressed moods, frequent tearfulness, appetite disturbances, mood swings, and challenges bonding with their babies. In addition, PPD is also often characterized by high anxiety levels and sometimes by panic attacks or obsessional thoughts. Some women with PPD can experience thoughts of harming themselves or their babies, or have recurrent disturbing thoughts about their babies.

"If you notice these symptoms in yourself or in someone that you care about, it is important to seek help as soon as possible. Postpartum Depression support groups, psychotherapy, and psychopharmacology have all been shown to be helpful. Organizations (like Postpartum Support International), your OB-GYN, or even your child's pediatrician may be a great resource for finding a referral for treatment of postpartum mood issues. In addition to affecting the way you are feeling, postpartum mood disturbances can affect your ability to bond with and care for your baby, lead to conflicted relationships with family members, and get in the way of achieving your personal and professional goals. Women can sometimes feel reluctant to seek out mental health care during this time. However, receiving treatment when you need it has the powerful potential to improve your mood and help you to be more engaged and effective as a mother, partner, and professional."

Even when our kids start sleeping through the night, no one ever tells us why they still periodically wake up. Here's the many reasons why my five-year-old often wakes up in the night: he is coughing, he had a bad dream, he doesn't like his bed anymore, there is a monster in the room, he needs water, when he was three he couldn't find his pacifier (yes, the pacifier obsession held on for quite a long time!), his blanket is rolled up around him, etc. Kids are little people and they will wake up needing you. There are things we cannot control (like two-month-olds needing to nurse and five-year-olds having periodic nightmares) and, my dear friends, there are things we *absolutely* can control. Pay attention.

I recognize that I may ruffle a few feathers here, but let me first return to the thesis of this book: if we do not care for ourselves, we cannot become the creative and productive women we long to be. Which is why we're reading this book, right? I am an extremely devoted mama. I run to my children when they need me. We snuggle often. But when it comes to sleep, we have boundaries in our household. Once we pass infancy, children sleep in their own bed. We sleep in ours. When my son has been ill, I have slept with him on a pull out bed in *his room* so as not to confuse the fact that sleep in our household is a solo activity. I know there are plenty of families that promote co-sleeping for years on end, but I can't help but notice that it's many of these moms that still haven't gotten sleep back into their lives. And sleep is *key* to our mental health. I'm not interested in a debate as to the many reasons sleeping as a family is wholesome and the way villages used to operate. I'm merely arguing that sleeping as a pack is not the recipe for restful, uninterrupted sleep—for parent or child. Many highly productive individuals, Arianna Huffington for example, have written *books* about the importance of rest if we are to be productive people.

Again, if we have children, we will periodically be woken up. When they are tiny, we will have nightly feeds. When they are toddlers, they will watch *Thriller* and think there is a zombie in their room at three in the morning (or was that just my son?). But there is a certain point when we have more control than perhaps we think we do. I admit that letting my son "cry it out" was painful (more for me than for him, I think), but am I glad that he is a solid sleeper who knows how to sleep independently now? Yes. Am I glad that, minus illness and nightmares, I can depend on a solid stretch of sleep so I can be a productive person? I sure am.

Do not discount how sleep may affect your mental state. If your child is two months old and you are blurry with exhaustion, well, my friend, this is normal and this too shall pass. Breathe and accept the moment for what it is. But if your child is two and still waking you up through the night, I argue you have something to think about. Do you need help navigating funky sleep patterns? That's okay! There's help to be found—either through the in-person help of a sleep consultant, or the many books and articles to be found online. There's so much information and support out there. Don't be ashamed, but do challenge yourself. What can you do to create the best conditions for your solid mental state of mind?

Nutritional Needs for Your Mental Health

Our mental state can be affected by our physical state. When we have given birth, lost blood, and are nursing, we are often depleted of necessary nutrients. We also might need some extra support if our mental state and sleep is shaky. Read below from a knowledgeable *Beyond Mom* nutritionist, Priya Lawrence, on some of the vitamins, minerals, and hormonal supplements we might need to get our mind back on track and functioning optimally.

Tips from Priya Lawrence, MS, RD, CDN, registered dietitian nutritionist, co-founder of Tried and True Nutrition, Inc.

"So now what? You have just spent ten months of thinking about the best nutrition for you and your baby and now that the big moment has arrived, you may not be thinking about much other than swaddle blankets and pacifiers. I often hear from new moms that the concern about proper nutrition for mom takes a back seat when the priority becomes the many needs of the baby. Even for those who do prioritize a healthy diet, breastfeeding or not, it's not always easy to always keep it forefront.

"A healthy diet can be so beneficial to mom and baby almost immediately after birth but we need to enlist some help on being sure we can achieve it.

"Tips to achieve a healthy diet as a new mom:

1. You may be relying on help when you first come home from the hospital. Before having the baby, discuss what you would like from this help, whether it's cooked meals, diaper changes, over night help or grocery shopping. Do not assume it will come if it's not discussed in detail.

2. While you will be sleep-deprived and maybe craving sweets or junk, try to limit that for just a few days, or maybe a week. The less time you indulge, the faster you will heal and start feeling like yourself again. You need all the vitamins and minerals you can get to give to you and your baby.

3. Always drink water. Drink more water than you even think possible. I used to ask my mom to bring me a huge glass of water each time I sat down to breastfeed my newborn daughter. And we know how often that is.

4. Do not wait until you are starving to eat. Often as a new mom, we forgo our immediate needs, but eating when we are starving means we most likely have low blood sugar. In which case, we are more likely to make a poor food choice and go for

something with some instant gratification (sugar), and we don't need that.

 Eat fruits and vegetables like they are going out of style. Your body needs anti-inflammatory foods, it needs antioxidants, and it needs Vitamin C to promote healing. Particularly if you have had a C-section, the Vitamin C foods are great to increase. The best way to know you are getting these is to increase all vegetables and fruits."

"Foods with these particular properties are:

Anti-inflammatory foods: green leafy vegetables, nuts, salmon, olive oil, strawberries, oranges

Antioxidant foods: broccoli, blueberries, strawberries, grapes, leafy greens

Vitamin C: citrus fruits, broccoli, salmon (also great source for DHA), nuts, seeds, sweet potatoes

Calcium and Vitamin D: dairy can be tricky for new moms as it is often what we are told to take out of our diets if the baby is fussy. Studies have shown milk has little to no effect on a baby's level of discomfort or 'fussiness' unless there is a real milk protein allergy.

However, just because studies don't prove any correlations, does not mean that we have all heard many people say the opposite and some will swear that by taking out dairy, the baby is less fussy. So, if you do or do not eat dairy, you will need to find a way to get calcium and Vitamin D and luckily it's not difficult.

Non-dairy foods high in Calcium: white beans, salmon, sardines, kale, almonds, oranges.

Non-dairy foods high in Vitamin D: tuna, salmon, egg yolks, and foods fortified with Vitamin D such as orange juice and cereals."

Acupuncture, Massage, and Exercise

The *Beyond Mom* methodology is built around making time for self-care to keep ourselves in a good mental space. When we are not mentally where we would want to be, self-care becomes even more imperative. There is something very powerful about loving ourselves enough to nurture, body and mind. It's like taking yourself by the hand and saying, *I believe in you, dear one, I'm going to do what I can to make you strong and happy again.* If money is of concern, get creative. Find acupuncture and massage schools that give low-cost treatment. Exercise, we discussed in the prior chapter. Where there's a will, there's a way.

But the benefits of these modalities aren't just "feel good." The reasons are quite scientific. Read below why acupuncture, massage, and exercise are extremely powerful tools when returning to a more balanced state of mind post-baby.

"As a mom and a woman, I'm on a constant journey to better myself, to be better for my family, and to learn new things. Be it new regimens of self-care (such as taking an impromptu pottery class or going to yoga), attending seminars or roundtables on the issues I'm most passionate about (like food and health), picking up an ingredient I've never worked with before, or getting my family started on composting. It's empowering to push ourselves and see just how much we can actually achieve when we try. I hope to impart that feeling of self-empowerment and belief that we can achieve whatever we put our mind to onto my son."

**—Ashly Yashchin, mother, health supportive chef,
founder of Barley + Oats**

High Nutrient Food

After my son was born, I bled like nobody's business. And it didn't seem to stop. A reality that many new mothers don't anticipate. Unlike most nursing mothers, I also returned to my monthly menstrual cycle within one month of giving birth. Not surprisingly, I felt totally depleted, not just physically, but mentally as well. I felt lightheaded and irritable. I realized quickly that I needed high nutrient food and I needed it quick—and easy. I started sautéing bunches of kale—nothing fancy about it. Kale, olive oil, salt, and fresh garlic. I ate hard boiled eggs. I made peanut butter and jelly sandwiches. I drank lots and lots of water. I asked those around me to help me cook. Before long, I felt myself more grounded both physically and most notably, mentally. Do not discount the power of nutritious food—it can steer our mental state from the darkest doldrums upward toward the brightest sun.

Sex

Let's talk about it. Sex, for me, post-child, was a delicate subject. I'll admit that in the three months post-childbirth, I wanted nothing to do with it. My nether regions had been through enough. But as time went by, I began to feel a longing for a sexual relationship with my husband again and started feeling sad that it wasn't part of the picture. Chatting with most new moms, sex is often non-existent for a certain period of time. Lack of sleep, stitches God knows where, and poopy diapers don't exactly create the mood . . . and yet, we are emotional human beings, and at some point, we need to *connect*. As we know, sex creates its own unique cocktail of hormones that give us the *I love you* feeling and can bring us back into our bodies and our sensuality, which is super important when our worlds have been turned upside down. When I think of the many reasons we feel mentally off during the year after having our babies, difficulty connecting with our partner sexually can rise to the top of the list.

"After having a baby, so much changes on varying levels within you. Your mind feels different, your body is not quite your own, and your spirit could be either soaring or low, depending on the day. All these components that make you the unique person you are, have altered, and there is a period of rediscovery. It's during these moments that I think healing modalities can really make a huge impact on your overall well-being. It's a moment for you. A moment to recalibrate. A moment to be still within yourself and receive, which is particularly special for a postpartum mom constantly in a state of giving. Let's not forget to mention the lack of sleep for new moms, which influences the ability to feel grounded, calm, energized, and present.

"While on the table of an acupuncturist, massage therapist, chiropractor, or any healer—there's space to quiet the mind, body, and spirit, and in that quiet, things can positively shift within and help a new mom discover what she needs without having to think so hard about it. It can just happen. Also, if there is pain or discomfort in the body (headaches, neck/back pain, GI disturbances, feeling sick, anxiety, hormones) these modalities can make a huge impact and offer pain relief, emotional calmness, and balance. And when these shifts happen (small or big), there comes momentum of change, of grounding, of confidence that inspires a woman to remember 'I can do this' or simply feel like herself again.

"On a personal note, I didn't reach out for help after the birth of my first daughter, and I was struggling. I forgot how to take care of myself because everything was about someone else. Even as someone in the healing world and knowing so many different amazing people, I didn't reach out. And somewhere at month eleven postpartum, I 'woke up.' I realized it was time to reach out. I immediately had acupuncture, saw a physical therapist that specializes in postpartum women's issues and saw a Pilates instructor who helps with diastasis. And when all of those things came together, I was able to slowly weave myself back into a person that felt in her body, strong, connected, and understood. Both because of the healing I was receiving, but also connecting to a community that understood what I was going through.

With the birth of my second daughter, I utilized these healers and others immediately within weeks, after learning from my mistakes. And having my team of healers at the ready made for a profound and immediate easier transition in myself that spilled over and made my family feel as a whole happier and more connected to each other amongst transition.

Figuring out what healing modality would fit your needs best depends on a few things—are your needs immediate or long-term, is there a healing goal, and do you have pain (acute/chronic)? If having an hour that is only yours in a dark, quiet place with minimal talking and healing touch sounds appealing, then massage therapy would be a good choice. Depending on where you go and the therapist doing the massage, your experience can be more spa-like or therapeutic. It's a great overall stress reliever and for many people, can feel like a mini escape. It can address pain issues; however, some people may find the post-massage results to be shorter lasting than other healing modalities like acupuncture or chiropractics.

If you feel like you need a more holistic approach to your health and well being, then seeing an acupuncturist may be a better fit. If you are experiencing acute or chronic pain, acupuncture will address the pain on both a physical and emotional level. This can often lead to longer lasting results. You and your acupuncturist will talk beforehand about your state of being, and then you will lie on a table and receive acupuncture. Often people find it very relaxing and a place to let go. Herbs, and nutritional and lifestyle advice are also part of your experience. Depending on your health goal, your acupuncturist will want to see you weekly or every other week."

—*Debra Ross, acupuncturist and herbalist*

remember about three and a half months after my son was born, I finally asked my husband why he wasn't trying to have sex with me. He admitted that he was scared of hurting me and that kind of killed the vibe. I told him I wanted to try, even though I wasn't sure how it would feel. In the following week, when the moment didn't present itself, I felt my confidence and my mood plummeting—maybe he just wasn't into it. And then, out of the blue, one afternoon while our son napped, we found our moment. It was patient and slow and, for the most part, felt good. But the best part was that I felt connected to my husband again, on both a physical and emotional level. My state of mind immediately lifted. I was still *here*. *We* were still *here*. Don't underestimate the power of sexual connection, physically and emotionally, to bring us back to who we are.

Finding it difficult to find your mojo post-baby? Two simple *Beyond Mom* suggestions . . .

It's likely you and your partner haven't had a free moment to be adults together. Can you sneak away for one hour and have a glass of wine at local bar? If not, can you reserve that hour after baby goes to sleep to put on mellow music and talk about anything that is not parent-related? The point is that you have to find the ability to reconnect with the spark that brought you together originally. It's very difficult to find your mojo if you can't do this. As a *Beyond Mom* who just had her third child said to me recently, "We went out to dinner last night and I remembered, 'I *like* Matt!'" In the case of my husband and I, we've discovered that we don't need hours to reconnect (though it's nice when that happens). We often only need a short dinner or a walk in the neighborhood to feel that connection once again—it's about quality, not quantity. If you haven't found those moments, don't be surprised if it's difficult to get sexy.

Do you need some new undies? I say this half jokingly, but not really. I remember after my son was born, I was still wearing the giant grandma undies that fit diaper-sized pads. Oh yeah, and nursing bras. Hot. I remember the day I went and bought myself a pretty matching underwear and bra set when my son was only three months old. I hadn't lost the baby weight yet, and my breasts were clearly their "nursing size." That set doesn't fit me anymore, but I'm so happy I bought myself something that made me feel pretty at that transitional time. And I remember it made me feel good knowing I had it on under the dress I wore the evening we went out for our first date night. Take responsibility for your own state of mind when engaging with your partner—is there something simple you can do to bring your own sexy back?

Sugar Mindfulness

There was a particular day when my son was a baby and in the phase of only napping in his stroller when it was moving, so I'd been walking for what seemed like forever. I'd left my house unprepared, and I was *hungry*. I strolled right past the health food stores and found myself at a French bakery, simultaneously moving the stroller to keep my son asleep, and shoveling a chocolate croissant into my mouth. While I enjoyed it, I look back and realize how nutritionally empty that was and, even more specifically, how much I abused sugar during that time. I had little time, I still had cravings (hello hormones) and, frankly, sugar is addictive, so I kept eating it. But just like sugar takes us on an insulin roller coaster that leaves us feeling exhausted, it also depletes us emotionally. So if we are serious about feeling balanced on all levels, we need to make sugar occasional and not frequent.

Looking back, if I would simply have taken time to pack myself some snacks in the same way I pack them for my son, I would have set myself up for success. I'm thinking of snacks like almonds, raisins, kale chips, bananas, or even a granola bar. Throw them in the baby bag so you don't get caught off guard with low blood sugar and end up grabbing something easy but unhealthy. If I could go back, I would take the time to make myself a meal—some scrambled eggs, some toast, something that holds me so the only thing shaking is the stroller.

It's so hard to take care of ourselves in the way that we do our children, but if we want to do this *Beyond Mom* thing right, it's imperative. Trust me.

Staying Nourished & Energized in the Postpartum
by Ashly Yashchin, mother, health supportive chef, and founder of
Barley + Oats

"Postpartum care is incredibly important, and next to rest (which can be hard to come by with a newborn), a big part of that boils down to proper nourishment. It can be hard to truly nourish ourselves with meals and snacks that contain the micronutrients we need to feel our best, especially when we are breastfeeding around the clock, sleep-deprived, and covered in spit-up.

"But proper nourishment inclusive of specific foods and herbs not only helps us heal faster, but also assists in our breastfeeding success, keeping our moods and energy stable, and helps us lose the baby weight without any sort of dieting or hunger pains. Luckily, there are a few easy tricks you can employ to stay nourished and energized in the postpartum.

"**Stock up the pantry and freezer before labor.** We've all heard this one. Stock your freezer with a bunch of lasagna, load the fridge with yogurts, and the pantry with granola bars. But I recommend taking this a step further. If you're going to take the time to stock up, choose the foods that provide the most nourishment with the least effort. One must-have in my pre-postpartum freezer is bone broth. It contains a lot of collagen, a protein found in the connective tissues of the body, skin, hair, and nails, and is responsible for strong, flexible bones, supple skin, and joint health.

"When it comes to the fridge, I recommend skipping the dairy if you're breastfeeding, at least for the first few weeks. Lactose and casein, the sugar and protein found in milk, can be hard for a newly forming digestive system to process and can cause digestive distress (and a lot of tears) for baby. Almond, rice, or coconut milk work great, especially if you can find some cold-pressed kinds without the added fillers. Other great items to stock the fridge with: smoked salmon (rich in Omega-3,

DHA, and EPA, which pass through breast milk and help baby's brain development), hummus (lactogenic and protein-rich), kombucha and raw sauerkraut (great for helping get digestion back on track), pastured hard-boiled eggs (a great source of choline, which helps with baby's memory and learning), and organic roasted chicken (if you're breast-feeding, you may be starving those first few weeks, and chicken can get you through without eating your arm).

"Solicit help from friends and family. Let them organize a meal train. Accept your mother-in-law's offer to come over and cook and let you nap. When people ask if you need anything, say 'yes' and ask them to bring you some food. Trust me, you won't regret it.

"Sign-up for a meal delivery service. Even if it's only for the first few weeks postpartum, a meal delivery service can be a godsend in those early days. There are plenty of healthy, whole food–based options out there now—go for one that's fully prepared; even the Blue Apron's out there are going to require more energy than you have to give. Unless, of course, your partner feels up to the task.

"Take your vitamins. Usually the same regimen as your prenatal care should suffice. For me, that meant a high-potency probiotic, fish oil pills, and a prenatal multi.

"Drink your juice, or even better, chew that smoothie. Fruits and veggies are potent sources of the micronutrients you need to feel your best post-pregnancy. Juices and smoothies are not only super easy to make (throw it all in the blender and you're good) but packed with vitamins and minerals.

"Use the internet! Need groceries? Order them online. Want takeout? There's an app for that. Technology is your best friend in the postpartum: let them come to you.

"Give yourself a break! Need to chow down on a pizza pie one night? Enjoy it and move on! There is no room for guilt in the postpartum. Leave that mental energy for positive thoughts. Just try to compensate with some extra fruits and veggies the next day."

"Why might you be craving sex after giving birth? For all the same reasons you loved sex before the blessed event, plus some. In our desire to come back home to and feel deep connection with our bodies after pregnancy and birth, rediscovering and recommitting to sexual pleasure is a worthy practice.

Sex, and solo self-pleasure, bring with them the physical pleasure, relaxation, and balancing hormones new mamas need.

Oxytocin, the bonding hormone normally associated between mother and infant, can also reconnect new parents who will probably feel the stress and strain of a new person in the relationship to take care of. This powerful 'cuddle hormone' also creates trust and generosity, which parents need to get through the challenges of early infancy.

Sex and self-stimulation also release a symphony of other hormones in the perfect amounts. Endorphins, natural pain-killers, are definitely healthier than a handful of Advil for post-labor pains. They also act as mood boosters and stress relievers, which can help with minor cases of postpartum depression.

Many doctors recommend waiting six weeks after delivery before having sex again. My midwife made no such pronouncement, although I had some major stitches to heal from! Her recommendation was to do what felt good for my body and not push myself further than felt safe. I was encouraged to start with gentle self-pleasure as a way to reconnect to my body and find physical pleasure in the long days and nights of early motherhood."

**—Alexandra Jamieson, Author of *Women, Food, and Desire*,
co-creator of Super Size Me, and host of Her Rules Radio**

Is Your Life Buoying You Up—Or Pulling You Under?

I remember a time when life was simple, when my biggest problem was whether a boy called me or not, or if I had a top I liked for Friday night. Maybe I'm oversimplifying. I can't say I would swap the drama of my teens and twenties for the maturity and clarity of my thirties, but I admit there are days when I long for a life that doesn't feel so complicated. Let's face it: *adulthood isn't easy*. Once we get into the world of employment, self-employment, committed relationships, and of course, the big kahuna, KIDS, life is never simple again.

Life with a family is hard. What I want to discuss are the reasons why, in early family life, we sometimes feel like it's *so* hard. It might not be at all what we thought we signed up for, but I've got some helpful suggestions for how to navigate this rocky and very real terrain.

The ultimate goal: getting back to a sense of mental clarity from which to achieve productivity and motivation.

I'm working on bringing you back to a state where pursuing your dreams feels tangible.

Not sure if I'll get backlash for this one, but I'll take a risk. I think today's society likes to encourage women to be just like men. And, after the many conversations I've had with hundreds of achievement-oriented women, I would like to state what to me is an obvious fact: men and women are not the same. We are capable of the same things, and should be entitled to exactly the same opportunities. But we operate differently. As women, and especially mothers, we operate emotionally and we need our foundation (our kids and partners) to feel rock solid under our feet. If things are shaky, it's hard for us to focus, and I think it's okay to admit that. Does it set us back from achieving our dreams? Not at all. What it does mean is that we need to tune in to the parts of our lives that might be weakening our foundation. We need to be very honest about our personal lives so that our productivity becomes assured. The successful women in my *Beyond Mom* community have found some kind of recipe that works, and it's generally inclusive of time with their partner and time for themselves. Basically, they invest time in making sure their family life and sense of self are as solid as possible. One might think productive women don't have time for such things, but what is overlooked is that it is *because* that time is carved out that these women *can* produce.

Taking all of this into account, another note from Terri Cole (can you tell that I love this woman's wisdom?):

"The truth is—what do you have to actually give if you are not nurturing yourself in some way, and ultimately you will become martyred. It's inevitable. If your self-care is bad, you will give and give and give and give, and in the beginning it feels okay, and then, by the end, you become the parent who is like, 'I gave up my youth and my beauty for you.' You literally become that person."

So let's get back to the early days of motherhood and how you can begin to put these things into practice when, let's face it, the realities of family life are hitting you square between the eyes.

How Are You Getting Along With Your Partner?

I remember when I was pregnant, my husband held my arm with extra care when crossing the street, brought me snacks in bed, and would speak to our unborn child in a way that melted me. But when baby arrived, that connection fizzled away and we started to battle. Over what, you may ask? The truth: I hated the way he did things with our newborn and I couldn't help but correct his every move. My hormones were raging and the exhaustion was debilitating, and so I resisted his demand to figure it out with our son. He told me he had to have room to make mistakes so that our son could trust him, too. At the time, mama lioness didn't want to hear it, but, in retrospect, my husband was totally right. I did have to step aside and let him figure it out.

It took a few months to work through all the physical changes I was going through and the emotional ones we both were experiencing. Looking back, I see that those were rough times for us. What helped us? Something we call "couch talk." It's a sacred time, that either one of us may request, to sit, focus, and have the difficult conversations. We practiced this from the beginning and utilized this skill to carry us through these rough times. The ability to sit down face-to-face, talk, listen, cry, or curse, well it's what makes or breaks a relationship. We all need to hear and be heard. Are you and your partner communicating since the child has been born? Or do you feel more like two ships passing in the midnight feeding? Do you need to air out some dirty emotional laundry? It's likely you do.

Back to my point: as women, we need our relationships to be grounded to feel like we can soar. Investing time in much-needed communication is exactly what the psychologist ordered and will give you a sense of freedom in your other pursuits.

How is Your Support System?

Another common misconception is that we can do this motherhood thing alone, and we should simply know what to do. Can you imagine taking the SATs without any preparation? Getting set loose in a kitchen without ever having read a single recipe? Why would parenthood come without some assistance? Living in NYC, there are a million resources—lactation consultants, physical therapists, nutritionists, counselors, and yet, such a vast majority of women think they *should be able to manage solo*. That *good mothers* just innately

"If you're feeling overwhelmed, exhausted, or frazzled, the first step to more balance and sanity might be giving yourself permission to prioritize self-care, and the next is strategically figuring out how to make it happen regularly. This requires carving out sacred time in your calendar to go to the gym, see pals, write, create, or do whatever it is that lights you up. Getting your partner on board is also an important part of this plan. Make time to sit down and share how you're feeling and why it's important to you, without approval-seeking. The more clarity you have, the more empowered you'll feel in the conversation. You can enlist help from family and friends, or swap hours with another mom pal. It may take time before the new normal feels comfortable, but it's worth the effort. Your authentic sense of satisfaction will positively impact all aspects of your life and by taking good care of yourself, you become a role model for how your children can do the same one day."

—Terri Cole, licensed psychotherapist, relationship expert, and founder of The Real Love Revolution

know these things. So much pressure we place on ourselves! Don't live in a big city? I assure you help exists in your hometown for whatever it is you struggle with— mothers are everywhere so their issues (and solutions) follow close behind. Can't afford to pay for services? The internet is a powerful tool. Lactation consultants have You-Tube channels. The same goes for almost any other concern. Additionally, many hospitals, pediatrician offices, and family centers have new mother groups where you can freely bring up concerns and questions. We are not alone nor should we be. Sometimes I think the feeling that we should have it all figured out is exactly the thing that sets us up to fail. Admitting we don't know it all and need the support of other women allows us to be receptive to the people and information that will make our lives better.

> "Part of it is really realizing you're not that fragile. You are resilient as hell. You can do this, and control fear. Put your arm around your fear and be like, 'Hey, kid, it's you and me until the end of time,' because as long as we're breathing humans on planet earth, fear is going to be a part of the life. You just have to take the keys away from fear, so that you're driving the van, and fear is just in the back seat."
>
> **—Terri Cole, licensed psychotherapist, relationship expert, and founder of The Real Love Revolution**

What limiting beliefs do you possess around your own motherhood abilities? Can you open up to the support around you? Can you be proactive and find the support you need? Congratulate yourself for asking for it—you are creating the conditions for your own growth and success!

Do You Have Enough Time for Yourself?

Probably the toughest question of all—and the universal answer is, NO! What mother has enough time for herself? What I've realized is that it's never *enough*. It's about finding *just enough* to fuel myself. Most of us have only several hours per week to devote toward self-development, self-love, or plain old free time, so how do you make the most of it and let it fuel you? Here are some things that have helped me make the most of my ME time:

1. *I step away from my to-do lists.* I can't live without my lists. They exist on a notepad in the kitchen, in notes on my iPhone, and in basecamp—my project management tool for my business. And though lists help me survive, they can also strip me of my mental freedom. If I'm constantly staring at what I have to do, I will never have the chance to do what I want to do. And doing what we want to do allows our true spirit to rise up and speak to us—*essential* if we are working toward a more active evolution of who we are. So in certain moments of my week, I put the lists away and let myself BE—take a walk, work out, be with my friends, go shopping, read a book, garden, you name it. It's letting myself just float, just for a little bit, just enjoying the moment. It's very healthy and sometimes forgotten for those of us who are hyper-productive and who are Moms—we always have a million things to do. Step away, sister. Step away.

2. *Make my mellow time count . . . for real.* Brene Brown teaches about numbing time versus nourishing time. Any moment can be either of these, depending on how we choose to use it. Example: an appointment is unexpectedly cancelled and you're blessed with a free hour to yourself. Do you get a coffee and pick up your iPhone? Or do you grab that book you've been meaning to crack and peruse it over that cup of coffee? Let's break it down: the time on the iPhone (though it can be productive if you're returning work

emails) is still defined as *numbing*. You're not present with your *self* and you're certainly not pouring something new and creative into your mind. Picking up a book, or even a favorite design magazine, I argue is *nourishing* because you're engaging with something you enjoy, something that inspires you, and parts of your creative brain that might not be getting tickled. And who doesn't love a luxurious hour to pore over a magazine? Similar example: how many of us as moms cook food and simultaneously text, talk on the phone, put dishes away, etc.? Essentially, we are numb to the beauty of something as simple and powerful as cooking healthy food. Can each activity be more nourishing if we actually focus on it? Absolutely. In some ways, this is a curse of the day and age we live in. But we're talking about our mental health here, and the way to get the most out of each moment in our life is to keep asking ourselves, are we numb or are we nourished? You have the power to choose what you want each moment to be. I admit, as a busy mom and entrepreneur, this one is a challenge, but I'm telling you, my morning cup of tea is so much more blissful gazing out at the snow falling than it is scrolling through my Facebook feed.

Some tips for finding ME time,
from some of my go-to experts:

"How
do you reel it in and
actually find sanity and find time for
yourself? I find that if you can just take a pause,
even if it's when everybody is asleep or if it's just taking
an afternoon and grabbing lunch by yourself, or scheduling that thirty-minute appointment with yourself to create space, breathe in the universe, just so you can step back and ponder what really matters right now . . . what really, really matters, with your life right now? For me, I reflect on the roles I embody: I'm a mother, I'm a partner, I'm a daughter. I own a business. I have a career. What really needs my time right now? What really needs to change a little bit?'

"Maybe you feel like you've been slacking on the food you've been giving your child. Maybe you've been slacking on a date night with your husband because you've been arguing. I find that when I can create this space to check in and simply ask, 'Are my actions aligned with what really matters?' it is really transformational to how you can stay on top of things in the right way."

—**Claudia Chan, founder of SHE**
Global Media and SHE
Summit

"I call it my happy place, and that happy place means spending time with me. I often say that I am no good to anybody else, not even my fourteen-year-old, if I am not whole within, if I am not at peace with myself, and how do I find that? I find that in nature. I proceed knowing that I am guided and God is there, and because of that I have unlimited energy to go out to create."

—**Alene Mathurin, author and founder of My Nanny Circle**

"You know when you get on the airplane and the crew says 'In the event of an emergency, put your oxygen mask on first before assisting others.' That's kind of my life mantra. There is not a day that goes by that there's not some form of self-care. People ask me how I find the time—you make the time. You make yourself a priority. If I don't take care of myself, I'm not going to be able to take care of my daughter, my husband, my household, my clients. Sometimes it feels like sneaking in time. If I'm on the subway headed to a meeting, I take the time to listen to a favorite podcast. I finish up my to-do list a little quicker than usual if I know there's a yoga class waiting. Just carving out fifteen minutes to call a friend and catch up makes me a better person, so that's really why I will always find the time."

—**Jenny Powers, founder of Running With Heels and podcast host of Broad-Cast: Broads Building Businesses**

The Emotional Tsunami—What Is It and How Do I Surf?

As moms, we come to rely on certain things—or certain people—working properly or showing up. We rely on our partners, our caretakers, our friends and family, even the schedule we create for our children. We rely on the stroller not jamming, the car seat not breaking, and the nearest grocery store to keep stocking our child's favorite pouches/biscuits/instant grains. Naptime is another key part of our foundation. It's when we rejuvenate, or simply just fall asleep ourselves. The people that help care for our children (be it our husband or the teenager next door) give us those moments of freedom to look forward to and, frankly, make our load a little lighter.

But in the great stretch of motherhood, it is best to expect the unexpected. Are things ever how we imagined them to be? Most women are shocked at how difficult nursing actually is and confounded by how difficult age three is as opposed to the typical *Terrible Twos*! Things are never exactly how we imagined them.

In many of these unexpected instances, I experience what I call *the emotional tsunami*—or the flooding response to something that we think should be unfolding in another way. For certain, hormones and lack of sleep only accentuate this response. But I've learned some serious lessons of my own on how to better manage and recognize what some of these emotions are *really* about.

I remember several years ago when my little one was just walking, my husband, who travels quite a bit for work, learned that he would have to be away over the Memorial Day weekend. I don't know what happened to me, but looking back, I'm certain it was an *emotional tsunami*. I became angry and resentful—frankly, pissed off that he would be leaving us during a holiday weekend. I was bubbling over with anxiety—what would I do with my little guy, all by myself, for a long weekend? We would be at our upstate weekend home, so this made me feel even more removed from our New York City reality, where we tend to have a little more going on. Any friends we might turn to for company would be busy with their own families, I assumed. My husband took the "you guys will be just fine attitude," which only angered me more. If I weren't a mom, I'd think this reaction was excessive, but I assume most moms will understand what it feels like to be told that you will be solo with your eighteen-month-old in the country for four days. EEK!

As the weekend rolled around, I got myself prepared. I stocked up on both our favorite foods, and began to call the few family friends I thought might be around. When the weekend arrived, my husband traveled up with us and helped settle us in. When he left, I bit my tongue, trying not to say anything negative. This probably avoided a giant fight prior to his departure (which wouldn't have done anyone any good). Time began to slow down for my son and I. We took walks to the pond and watched ducks, frogs, and dragonflies for an hour. We told stories about worms in the dirt. We inspected our tomato plants. We threw rocks into the Hudson River. We snuggled and watched a little more TV than usual. Surprisingly, friends weren't too busy for us and we were invited to several Memorial Day barbeques and play dates. This unexpected holiday weekend with my son ended up becoming some of the sweetest time we had ever spent together. Was my initial reaction excessive? Maybe. But I definitely understand how these emotional reactions arise so furiously for mamas. Our emotional stability is so often dependent on our schedule and, of course, on our major relationships, and like everything else, we can't always control these external forces. But if we're working toward having a positive and proactive relationship with our life, we have to learn to work with these moments in a way that is clear and rational. Let's discuss.

What You Can Do to Accept What You Cannot Change

In life, it's easy to lose it and blame realities in our lives on something else, instead of owning our relationship to it. Many people function in this way 100 percent of the time. And these are not generally our favorite people to hang around, nor some of the most positive or productive people we know. Emotional Tsunami is totally normal. Getting slammed by it for long periods of time? Not pretty—and not the platform for forward motion. Let's discuss helpful tips to mindfully navigate these moments. I'll use my above story of finding out my husband's traveling over Memorial Day weekend as an example.

1. **Slow down your immediate reaction.** When my husband told me he would be traveling over Memorial Day weekend, I quickly wanted to give him the "are you F-ing kidding me?" response. I wanted to guilt-trip him and make him feel like a bad father and husband. Would these reactions have gotten me anywhere? Nope. They would've definitely sent me way back into the emotional doldrums. I've learned over time that many of my emotional tsunamis are made twenty times worse by verbally acting on them the moment I feel them flooding in. If you need to simply nod your head and take a few moments to yourself, do so. Just don't speak before you've had time to process.

2. **Ask yourself what it's really about.** Often, when we take the time to slow down and process our feelings, we can figure out what our emotions are actually about . . . and often it's not what we think. In my case, I immediately felt abandoned by my husband and resentful of having my son all those days solo. When I slowed down, I realized I felt embarrassed that my husband would be away during a holiday weekend. My family taught me that families should be together for holiday weekends, and most evenings—a bit of a traditional approach. When I really dug deep, I recognized that we aren't a traditional family and 95 percent of the time, I'm okay with that! We work with what we've got and come together meaningfully in all kinds of ways, but it's not always according to a specific calendar. I had to get over that sense of shame and embarrassment that came from my old mental tape player.

3. **Remind yourself that you are stronger than you think.** So often we react because we think we can't pull it off and we *need* something . . . or else we will fall apart. Every single time I have been caught off

guard in a moment with my child, I have surprised myself with my ingenuity and creativity. They haven't always been easy moments, but I have come through stronger and more confident than before. Our ego loves to tell us how weak and incapable we are, but reality is generally something else entirely. We need to recognize our individual capabilities so that our fears don't make that tsunami wave even higher and more devastating when it crashes.

But this also illustrates a bigger point, which is that we are capable of using our own mindfulness tools. These tools can be applied to any of the unexpected turns during motherhood—nursing difficulties, relationship battles, even questions about getting back to your work life.

- Can you slow yourself down and be mindful about what's really going on?
- Can you discover your own tools to work through the angst as it arises?
- Most importantly, can you trust that you have the tools to navigate whatever may arise? You really are more powerful than you think, even more powerful than the giant wave overwhelming you.

If You Cannot Accept it, Change it

Okay, now that we've taken the time to slow down and ask ourselves what our emotional responses are *really about*, we can more accurately define that which is just emotional excess—and that which is our truth. What does the truth consist of? It is reality as it arises from our core, not from some frenetic, anxiety-ridden state of mind. It usually arises when we are calm and clear and have spent some time contemplating wherever we've landed. The great thing about coming to our truth is that we're no longer in a victim mentality and now we can take action.

Some examples of truth revealed:

1. If nursing has been more of a burden than you ever expected—you have not slept in weeks, your nipples are bloody and war-torn, and the sight of a pump makes you feel suicidal—your truth might be that you cannot go on like this any longer. But your truth might also be that you still want to nurse. Action from your truth might come in the form of an email to your mom friends to retrieve the names of a few trusted lactation consultants to get some assistance once and for all. Another mom's truth might be that she is DONE nursing. Her action might be to order some organic formula and put the pump back in the closet. Both decisions came after taking a few quiet moments to contemplate what is really going on emotionally (and physically) and navigating from that place. No victims here—only proactive choices for everyone's greater good.

2. After my husband took the Memorial Day trip, I discovered that if I embraced unexpected moments with my son, I would likely have a predominantly positive experience. But my truth was that I still don't love for my husband to travel over long holiday weekends. We discussed this and he assured me that he would do his best to avoid it in the future.

3. Feeling overwhelmed by full-time motherhood? Feeling the nudge of creativity and the itch to "do something?" Can you slow down, acknowledge the feelings, ask what they're really about, and perhaps do some journaling over what is coming up for you? Are you needing some more babysitting help so you can begin to contemplate your next steps? Or is it enough to begin jotting down ideas and dive in when your child starts preschool?

There's no wrong answer. There's only a process. Do you want that process to be painful and directionless? Or do you want it to be mindful, clear, and decisive?

Moving toward a *Beyond Mom* life requires next level attention to your emotional highs and lows and a deep dialogue with the fragile parts of yourself. It takes a little more work up front, but, trust me, the result is a path that's clear and better supported. From here, you will be going places.

When the emotional tsunami is real, know that you will survive it.

There are moments in our lives, in anyone's life, when the unexpected occurs. Loved ones pass away, relationships break apart, illnesses descend upon us. In our current case, we can't just give in to our emotional upheaval and stay in the thick of it, swimming in a pool of our own shock, sadness, anger, or whatever emotions have arisen! Our little ones need us and depend on our stability. Many of the same skills apply here that we discussed in relation to our personal emotional tsunamis. We must give room for the feelings, in this case, we might need to find personal spaces to let them out where our children are not affected. These feelings, I've discovered, do need room to air out so the key is to find safe, private space to release them. The next important step is to find the support system you need to keep you afloat. This can range from close friends, cousins or siblings, or professionals that specialize in the field of loss or illness. Your family needs you so you must care for *you*, even if it feels like the time or resources aren't there. We live in a virtual world, so by all means, join chat rooms and Facebook groups dedicated to the issue you're contending with and find the voices of those who can really understand your struggle. It feels so good to be understood. I'm also a really big believer in honesty with your kids. If you're going through something, tell them so. You don't need to over share or share details that are developmentally too much for your child to handle. But letting your child know that you're human and humans go through things is good for their overall development and embracing of their parents as real people (with flaws, successes, and losses too). And the most important tip I can offer you as you navigate the larger challenges in your life is to have faith in the foundation you have built for yourself and utilize the tools you know—health (mind *and* body), a community of loved ones and friends (more on that in the next chapter), and a faith in the strong individual that you are. Mothers have withstood challenges of all shapes and sizes, but we figure it out because we love our kids . . . and we love ourselves too (or at least we should).

I lost my father years before my kids were born, but the wound of that loss is still very real and to this day, can take my breath away. I rely upon the tools of mindfulness to acknowledge the sorrow when it descends upon me; I've been honest with my son since he was old enough to understand that my daddy isn't here . . . and I miss him. I've told stories about him so my son understands how fabulous a man his grandfather was, and that soothes me. I surround myself with friends who knew and loved my dad and even if friends didn't know him personally, understand the hole left in my heart. And most importantly, as painful as it's been to navigate life without him, through that pain, I have found some of my greatest gifts—compassion, ingenuity, and deeper love. I have become the woman I'm meant to be because through this loss, I was set loose into the messy, unpredictable world of womanhood. Just like me, my friends, you can navigate the hard stuff of life, with your kids in tow. Utilize your tools and their love to push you through.

"I think one of the hardest things being a new mom is being able to tune into your intuition. We've got to learn to trust our intuition. We've got to learn to stay connected to what's important to us and what we value, to what kind of children we want to raise, what kind of household we want to have and how we want the house environment to be. To remember that, especially as a mother, we set the tone for everything, and so being able to ground ourselves and calm ourselves down, gives us that strength to be able to make the decisions that are in alignment with our values and with our intentions.

"One of the things I teach people to do any moment when you feel stressed or when you feel like you don't know if you're going to make the right decision, (whether it's about breastfeeding, stopping breastfeeding, what food to feed, or when to put the kid to sleep, there's so many new things that are on our mind that we often feel so unequipped to deal with) is a practice called heart breathing. So if you find yourself stressed and worried, the best thing that you can do is to take thirty seconds to just pause. It can be when you're walking. It can be in the grocery story. It can be when you're driving. You don't have to be in a lotus position to do it. You tune and turn your awareness to the heart center, the area where the heart is and you imagine you have a mouth there and you breathe in and out through this heart center, through this space, and research shows what happens is that when you start breathing from the heart and you tune into it, it creates a coherence.

"We all know that when we make decisions from a stressed-out state, it actually causes more problems. So, when we want to make decisions that are important to us, we want to make sure we are making a decision from our heart, and not from our freak out, flight or fight state of mind."

—Patricia Moreno, fitness expert
and founder of IntenSati Method

"As a *Beyond Mom*, I do it all. There is a lot that doesn't come naturally, but I strive to make it look seamless. I view myself as a mother first and foremost, and everything after falls into place. I have always been independent with an entrepreneurial spirit, and despite juggling all my mama activities including shuttling my daughter to numerous extra-curricular activities, play dates, and volunteering at school, I have launched my new coaching business, I help my mother run our family's non-profit, and I try my best to stay connected to family and friends. My favorite quote by Walt Whitman sums up everything about me . . . 'Do I contradict myself, very well, then I contradict myself. I am large. I am multitudes.'"

—Hope McGrath, mother and life coach

CHAPTER 3

Your Community within the Home

THIS IS LIKELY THE FIRST SMALL business you are going to run. It will not only break you in, but it will also give you the practice you need to command a ship and its fleet. As women, we can become emotionally overrun by what is required to care for our families, but I'd like to propose something that might seem a little radical . . .

- *What if we could first and foremost put our needs as a top priority?*
- *What if the time for self-care and idea cultivation becomes as equally important as doctors appointments and family dinner?*

If we could truly accept that the development of who we are as women is of grave importance to the health and well-being of the family, we might approach the entire discussion with more motivation, increased focus, and fewer apologies.

I am the first person to admit that finding an equation that works can be a challenge, so let's discuss what's involved in not only defining what you need in the community of your home, but also a variety of ways to get there.

What Is Your Home Community and Who's in It?

Your home community consists of anyone who enters the home and helps the machine of the family run smoothly by doing any of the following: childcare, cooking, cleaning, errands, and any extraneous schlepping or online ordering of stuff. These jobs are not meaningless. Ask any stay-at-home mom or dad how encompassing these tasks can be and how challenging it is if you are not on top of them. Having help with these tasks makes other parts of life more possible, whether that help comes from a relative or through hired support. Many of us view having help in some of these categories as spoiled or indulgent. Your home support community also consists of daycare if you utilize this mode of childcare as you must still manage your expectations and communication with those that care for your child.

For my readers struggling to ignite their inner spark, I urge you to consider the importance of this kind of support. There are only twenty-four hours in a day—how are you going to use them?

Your Partner—An Honest Discussion About the Home Community

The women who feel this *Beyond Mom* calling often find themselves at a difficult cross roads at this time in their lives. They have chosen to forsake an income to take time to be with their children, yet they've discovered they don't want an *or*—they want an *and*. But so many women feel guilty approaching their partners, asking for extra support in the home. "I'm paying a babysitter so I can go to a *spin class?*" women ask me. Yes, you are. Back to chapter 1, we need to feel grounded in our body to pursue any venture. "I'm having my mother-in-law come in two days a week so I can sit in a café and write?" Yes, that's precisely what you need to do. Just like a pregnancy, your ideas need a gestation period and you need space to cultivate them. The early stages of anything won't make money, but I guarantee you that in order to make money, you need the space to seed your ideas.

My client, Lynette, wanted to start a blog. Her goal was to be paid for her articles and she had the connections to make that possible, but simply lacked the time. She had stepped away from her editing position for an online magazine when her daughter was born, but quickly realized how much she had to say about motherhood and wanted to get back into the game—on her own terms. She tried to write during her baby's naps, but that quickly proved unpredictable and futile. She recognized she needed some babysitting help to make any of this possible, but felt guilty asking her husband to put any of their sole income toward the time it took for her to design a blog and write her articles—after all, this didn't result in any immediate income. But her husband knew her talent and wanted to see her happy so agreed to hire a babysitter two days a week for a six-month period while she developed her concept, took meetings with key connections, and got writing again. They both felt it was fair to revisit the conversation in three-month's time to see how things were shaping up. By the time the three-month discussion arrived, her blog was up and she was getting paid for some of the articles she was writing. Her return on investment revealed itself and she felt fabulous. Her husband was thrilled to see her creative life unfolding and they both agreed to keep the babysitter on.

Lynette didn't feel like she was asking for something. She expressed a desire to her husband and he recognized its importance. They figured out their budget for babysitting, how long they could sustain it for, and built their goals around it.

How can you create your own version of this story? How can you approach your needs and desires for growth with your partner in a way that is confident and clear? I urge you to remind your partner that you are an individual who has needs and ideas—you need time to cultivate you. This is not *selfish* in the negative sense. You need not ask permission here, you are merely explaining and exploring this new time in your life and asking to allocate some of the household budget for the support to do so. From there, you and your partner can explore the options.

If you're wasting energy selling him or her on your plan, you're not focused on steering. So step one is talking it through until you're in complete, supportive agreement.

What about when your work picks up and you need your husband to pitch in a little bit more around the house or with school pick up, as an example. These are the stressors and situations that can weigh on our shoulders, cause resentment if needs are unspoken, and generally create a counter-productive environment. I've come to realize that when the *mom* gets busy, the part-

The team perspective is essential. Your partner is your first mate.

ner that is simply used to mom being in the mom role feels a little lost. It's not that they are unwilling to contribute but that they need support in taking over some of the duties that were originally considered mom's. Trust me, I have destroyed many a moment with an attacking, resentful tone when I could've preserved peace by simply giving my partner the benefit of the doubt and speaking with kindness.

True story: my husband pitches in on the weekends with neatening up the house and will definitely tackle a sink full of dishes. I noticed that for some inexplicable reason he would leave behind all baby bottle parts in the sink, tackling only *adult* dishware and pots and pans. Why? I wondered. I had no answer, but only knew that seeing those remaining bottle parts made me feel oddly degraded, as if baby bottles are for women. My internal feminist began to rage. I had learned from previous encounters, however, how NOT to approach this situation. Attacking, accusing, assuming tones will get you nowhere fast. Asking questions with a level tone might get you somewhere. In this case, I simply asked him, "Hey babe, I really appreciate when you help out with the dishes but I notice you leave the bottle parts and other baby stuff in the sink and don't clean it. Is there a reason why?" Since I didn't attack him and asked him with room for him to explain, he did just that. He explained that the bottle parts were so small and he wasn't sure exactly how to clean them. He thought perhaps we (our caregiver and I) had our own method to cleaning them. "Nope," I told him. "No particular way, just the bottle brush, soap, and hot water, one piece at a time. Totally go for it!" The conversation ended there and the bottles haven't been left behind since. This is a small example of how our approach creates our reality. As *Beyond Moms*, it's in our power to approach moments with our partner with the end goal in mind. Do we want a supportive, involved partner? Yes. Then we must empower our partner by asking good questions, giving them room to figure things out (and that includes making some mistakes), and expressing our needs with clarity and compassion.

The Team

Now that we all agree that Mama needs some ME time . . . let's discuss how to create that home community that will give you the space you need to get yourself off the ground. Here I will address those that might typically enter the home and how to handle both the pluses and minuses of these relationships.

Mothers & Others

If your extended family of moms and mom-in-laws are unconditionally supportive, great, skip ahead. I admit that I'm jealous of my friends who have grandmas living nearby. The benefits are endless: school pickup, built-in babysitter, less guilt when traveling with hubby on vacation. Plus there's the added bonus of cultivating family closeness for your children. But if you have relatives in your home that are depleting you more than nurturing you, something has to change. And this dynamic is not always easy because, well, it's family.

Some women I know thought they had their future figured out when their mothers volunteered to babysit three days a week. *I'll be able to work out and begin designing my new website*, thought one mom.

Awesome. Fast forward six months and this same mom dreams of a home that feels energetically her own, and of a time when she felt like she made her own decisions for her child. This woman likely feels:

- undermined
- criticized
- silenced
- like an imposter in her own home

Don't despair. Remember, these are the difficult learning moments that are shaping the leader you will become in other aspects of your life. The microcosm of your home is the most important and imperative place to master the skills. So take a deep breath and consider what you would do in a professional environment if you felt any of these above emotions. Would you allow yourself to lash out with anger and tears? Probably not. It's more likely that you would formulate your perspective in an organized and clear manner, perhaps writing down notes about how you feel and examples of the moments those feelings arise. You would find a private moment when emotions aren't as high to sit down and clearly express your thoughts. With family, we tend to let loose whenever we feel like it. Remember, we have to cultivate our professional skills in our home environment, so give this version a try.

There is a truth I've learned and this truth holds water whether you're setting boundaries with employees or with family members. It's all in your voice. Yes, *your* voice. If you approach anything in a tone of weakness and insecurity, it's very easy to be walked over by someone who thinks they know better. My husband tells me that he can always tell when I'm speaking from my throat (a weaker place to speak from) or from my belly (the place we speak from when we are clear, calm, and confident). For me, speaking from this place has taken practice. It's like any muscle, with time and work it gets stronger. Think about how you speak to your family support inside your home. Do you ask their permission with a hint of insecurity (leaving them room to change the rules and tell you what you *should* do)? Or do you tell dear mother-in-law what you need her to do with a sense of grace and confidence (implying that you know exactly how to manage your life, child, and household). No one has to be mean here, but energetics are real and we need to own our territory.

To be clear, I'm not suggesting a know-it-all attitude and a consequential loss of support. I'm speaking to a deeper confidence that emanates from a deeper source. Can you see the difference?

And now the next question:

Are you getting nowhere fast? Does your mother-in-law bring the clash of a 1950s mentality into your modern and motivated home? You might have the most supportive husband this side of the Brooklyn Bridge, but your mother-in-law might pollute the space with snide remarks that disempower your efforts to have a life of your own. If this is the case, maybe Grandma is meant for Sunday afternoon play more than weekly caregiver. That decision is yours, but it's unacceptable to feel that your home values are taken over and especially that your voice is lost. *You* are the mama and the future entrepreneur, after all.

Caregiver decisions can be some of the hardest, especially if it's family. But own your space, own your family, and own your needs.

The Nanny and Other People Who Make Your Home Work

For many urban mamas and perhaps in other locales too, this may be your very first time being someone's boss. Within this extremely personal/professional relationship are endless opportunities for growth, both personally and professionally. For the sake of this discussion, I'm assuming that, as a family, you have determined that hiring help when managing your home and children makes the most sense. Maybe you live a plane flight from your immediate family or maybe you've determined that Grandma didn't make the best addition to your daily home life. You've put the budget aside to bring this person into your home to nurture and care for your most precious commodity—your child!

Our first nanny began working with us when my son was three months old. We have no family nearby, and I knew that I wanted time to cultivate my business life as well as be an active mom. We started at three days a week, but moved to four when *Beyond Mom* started to grow. Our nanny was definitely an integral part of our family life and flow.

When I became pregnant with our second child, I experienced a momentum starting in my work output, this book being a huge part of that. I started to look at the realities of my relationship with our caregiver and began to feel the need for a change. While she had an incredibly loving relationship with our son, I admitted to myself that she was what I would define as an unhealthy person. There always seemed to be something "wrong" with her physically, and her mood swings were unpredictable. I had numerous conversations with her about her own self-care and if I'm being totally honest, I accepted many things and swallowed too many feelings simply because I feared my son's reaction if we let her go.

One day, I read a quote that said that the momentum of your life is a direct reflection of the five people you see most often.

Whoa. That was a giant slap in the face for me. If our caregiver filled our home with strange, unpredictable energy, what did that mean for me, if I was absorbing it? As painful as it was, I decided that it was time to move on, that I was ready for a change, and my son would have to adjust. In this scenario, I confess that I was a complete mess for the weeks leading up to letting her go. I obsessed over the conversation, what I would say and how it would pan out. I organized myself as best as I could with a severance check and a speech. In this case, I kept it simple and for the sake of all involved, I didn't tell the complete truth.

You see, if the issue boils down to someone's personality, it isn't always something that can be discussed or absorbed, especially when emotions are running high. So I told her that our financial realities required us to assess childcare in a new light and that we wouldn't need full time support. She argued with me a bit, but I lovingly held my ground. In retrospect, I still may have said too much. I remember confessing how hard it was for me to imagine motherhood without her. At the time, that was my reality. Looking back, I recognize I just didn't understand the future possibilities for myself and for my family. It was an emotional conversation, but I did my best to keep it direct and relatively unemotional. And when she left, I had an intense belly cry, followed by a long shower in which I could just let it all out. I'm glad no one was home for that moment!

To date, it was one of the most painful "moving on" stories I've experienced, and even though in the end I followed my gut, I wish I could've come to my conclusion with a little less suffering. I do believe that's part of maturing as an adult and a businesswoman. Decisions become easier to make.

We now have a caregiver who embodies pure kindness and positivity—exactly what I want the top five people I see every day to exude. Many of the lessons I've learned as an entrepreneur have come through navigating our caregiver relationships and ultimate choices. Apparently, I'm not the only one!

Allison, a member of the *Beyond Mom* community, recently shared with me her struggle to communicate changes in her personal and professional needs with her son's nanny. She explained how her work life had really changed in the past year and that she needed more evening hours to network. Her nanny is paid during the fifteen hours a week her son is in school (I know to non-city moms this sounds insane, but it ensures availability for many busy urban families) but Allison started to wish that some of those "paid" hours could be transferred to a few weekly evening hours so she feels more available to get out and do her professional thing. She felt nervous discussing this concept with their nanny as she'd always been rigid about being paid for any extra evening hours. Allison also felt that she could use an extra hand with some food shopping and errand running while her son was in school, but she was unsure if she'd be willing. She came to me nervous and concerned and, yes, resentful because she felt like her nanny was the one in control. I could relate to this dynamic. We want harmony in our home and we want our child's caregiver to be happy as they are with our little ones day-in and day-out. And yet we cannot sacrifice our own needs. We must, as women and entrepreneurs, learn to speak with confidence and clarity.

I urged her to speak honestly with her son's nanny about the changes in her work life and the extra help she felt she needed. To her surprise, her nanny was willing to give her one evening a week in which the hours her son was in school could be applied. She was also willing to do some food shopping and other errands while her son was in school. Allison was happily surprised at the agreement they came to and really all it took was clarity of her own needs and the confidence to express them.

Important to note: if your child is in daycare, please don't disregard this section. You must also manage many of the same dynamics, communication skills, and boundaries as you would with someone in your home. So pay attention and read on!

Here are a few of the most important conclusions I've come to if you're going to engage with in-home community support . . . and these lessons hold true as you grow the *Beyond Mom* in you, too:

1. **Be clear with your expectations**
   As new Moms, we probably don't know how to cut our baby's fingernails or how to handle our baby's first fever. Often the more seasoned help around us gives us that important information, but don't let your inexperience as a mom be mistaken for lack of clarity of your expectations. If you expect your nanny to discuss the week ahead on Monday morning because it helps you feel organized, then speak that. If you need some help with cooking, ask your nanny if she minds fixing some simple food while the baby naps. If a positive

attitude is imperative to the vibe of your household, have a direct chat if you feel that the energy is a little negative. I've learned that I need to be clear with what I need or else no one will give it to me. I'm not talking dictatorship here, I'm talking confidence and honesty of what it takes to make the home space work. Share what your concept of this is—over and over again. Clear communication takes extra work upfront but it's an investment for the long haul.

2. **Write a contract**

My mistake when hiring our first nanny was not writing a contract. Putting everything in writing forces both of you to outline expectations in an organized fashion so no one is confused. The good news is that it's never too late to get clear, but I can't say enough how important this document is for everyone's peace of mind. And as an entrepreneur—you should *always* have a contract, whether with an intern, a freelancer, or a full-time employee. Everyone deserves clarity and guidelines. It makes the process so much better.

3. **Don't apologize for doing what you're supposed to do**

Many women find it challenging to tell someone, even someone who we pay, what we need them to do. I have had this challenge. Somewhere inside of me, I feel guilty asking someone to go out of their way. But I've had to simply get over this to build my own sense of self-confidence. I can always treat someone with respect and compassion, but I also deserve to ask the people that work for me to do what I need them to do! Where does this limiting belief come from? I'm unsure but I do know it's an all-too-common plague of the female species. Think of how far we can go if we remove those "issues" from our mind and proceed confidently inside of our home and in our businesses? Can we replace the undeserving messaging from our mind with words of empowerment for our work in our homes and beyond?

All this wisdom has bled into how I work with every person who supports the community of my home as well as my business. I now commit to clarity through contracts as well as frequent verbal communication. I no longer apologize for asking for what I need. Somewhere in this evolution of becoming a *Beyond Mom*, I've had to shed those habits which hold me back and keep me weak: worry, anxiety, guilt, and desperation. Instead, I commit to positivity, confidence, clarity, and honesty. Transitioning from one way of being to another has taken hard work and some profoundly challenging interactions, but I will say that the relationships that were born (or re-born) from this new version of myself are extremely healthy and rewarding for all parties.

Mastering these skills of communication and boundary setting will not just serve you as an entrepreneur . . . they are *imperative* if you're going to embrace the life of an entrepreneur (which, though rewarding, is not particularly easy).

I can assure you that managing your family life and those you allow in to help is an excellent learning tool for developing your voice and establishing a flow that works for you. Becoming a *Beyond Mom* isn't about being perfect. It's about setting an intention to create something from the part of you that is empowered. Your home community is the perfect fertile ground for planting the seeds for this new way of living.

Creating the culture of YOUR home (regardless of who enters it!)

❶ **Understand the culture of your home!** By identifying and knowing truly what the culture of your home is, what the philosophies are that are most important to you as a family unit, then you can begin to look at caregivers that have different skill sets and talents that can match the culture and dynamic of the family.

❷ **Emotionally prepare for what it's like to bring someone into your home.** I think even as Beyond Moms, moms that do so much, is the important recognition that somebody else is coming into the home and taking care of, and almost invading, that world she has created. Being emotionally grounded and secure to know that this person is coming in as a partner is key. So many times we forget there are emotional aspects of having somebody come into your home, and care for your child and take over your little area, your stuff, hugging and kissing your child, and that love being reciprocated. Moms need to recognize and emotionally understand the fact that we are bringing someone in to care for our child, and that it is not a reflection of our incapability but rather part of the process of creating whatever empire she is building.

—Alene Mathurin, author and founder
of My Nanny Circle, a community for caregivers

"One of the ways mothers in New York City and other places satisfy the need and longing for connection is they seek out a tribe of mothers they can relate to. We're looking for the other moms who we share philosophies with: what is your stance on crying it out? What is your stance on sleep training? What is your stance on using a sling or a baby carrier? How do you feel about strollers? There are dozens of tribal affiliations for different kinds of moms. I think the important thing is to find the group of like-minded men and women that you're comfortable with. Find the people who make you feel not only like a good parent, but also like you're capable of making good decisions and you're not being judged. That you're getting the help you need when you need it.

"In anthropology, the term for these people is 'alloparents.' The great socio biologist Robert Trivers came up with this term because he was observing other species and human beings. He saw other important individuals who aren't parents but are helping raise the offspring. He came up with the term 'allopaternal pair' to describe these special people. They're not actually your kin. They're not related by blood, but they're helping you out."

—Wednesday Martin, anthropologist and author of *The Primates of Park Avenue*

CHAPTER 4

Building Your New Community outside the Home

Acknowledging the Need

NO, MAMA, YOU CANNOT DO IT alone. And who told us that we should be able to? Historically, the core principles of raising a family revolved around community: aunties, grandmas, sisters, and friends. Everyone lived pretty much on top of one another. And, while that may have caused some space issues, it also provided built-in childcare, endless sources of information, and shoulders to cry on. Both of my parents were raised in Brooklyn in the 50s and 60s, living in the same apartment buildings as their immediate family. I've heard millions of hilarious stories over the years of what it actually meant to live on top of one another, but, beneath the surface, there is a story of unconditional support.

When the suburbs were developed in the post-war boom, these dynamics changed. For the first time, average people could afford *space*—but what did they give up? With larger homes and backyards came less immediate conversation in moments of frustration and less guarantee of childcare when you just need some personal time.

And where have we gotten at this moment in time? In many ways, we've taken major steps forward: women are encouraged to do anything, be everything, and are told they can do it all! We have online forums, websites, and meet-ups for moms who nurse, vegan families, and for kids with allergies. But where is the support for the deeper conversation? Who can you reach out to when the needs aren't so obvious (less *my boobs are killing me* and more *my soul is crumbling*)? Let me just state what I believe is a fact: as mothers and women, we must have community to survive. If we think we can tackle the strains of motherhood (and womanhood) solo, we are in for a pretty rude awakening.

The Multi-Faceted Purposes of Community within Motherhood

Once we are face-to-face with motherhood, we feel how real the need for support is. Men wonder how it's possible that we can bump into a woman in line at the supermarket and, in five minutes or less, know about their pending divorce, their hyperactive four-year-old, and their recent gluten allergy diagnosis. This is how we work, the female species. We get down to business and we connect fast. What do we need from each other most?

Solution Sources

Breast pumps, cribs, strollers, husbands—all these things malfunction from time to time and we need solutions. Other women have certainly been through some version of what we think is the world's greatest crisis. I personally love that, usually after just one or two conversations, I have some practical wisdom and clear direction on how to manage whatever my issue is. Women may be emotional, but we're also proactive. We help each other with the know-how to move through stressful moments and get to a better place.

Support and Validation

Is there anything better than the words, "I have totally been there, I know how you feel. I promise, you will get through it?" Recently, a dear friend who is generally very composed and mellow about parenting, texted me on a Sunday morning with the ultimate SOS: *I'm going to lose it.* I knew I had to get there fast. When I arrived, her three-year-old son was bouncing off the walls and her four-month-old was crying. Her husband was away for the weekend. Other than providing my three-year-old to exhaust her three-year-old, I didn't do much of anything for her in actuality. We talked, hugged, and sighed it out. After two hours, I headed back home and later she texted me telling me that I had saved her life. It doesn't take much. But the innate connection we share, the compassion for one another's struggles, keeps us all afloat.

It's also worth stating that motherhood can feel like an insane asylum more often than some of us want to admit. We just don't know if our "abnormal" is "normal." All it takes is one good conversation with another Mom to know that everything is okay and you and your children shouldn't join the circus. Oh, thank goodness for those conversations!

Joy Loves Company

Some of the old phrases of yesterday remain true today. Misery loves company, but I argue that joy does, too. The sleeplessness, the hormones, the complexity of shifting into life as a mom, well, we need someone to complain to. But the joys need the same attention. Moms love nothing more than sharing their camera roll with another passionate mama—we feed off each other's oohs and ahs, and we love to compare the cute things our kids say. This is part of the communal experience of motherhood highs and lows—don't forget to share the good stuff!

Health & Fitness

I love how women inspire one another. We not only offer suggestions ("Have you tried the amazing new juice shop on 14th Street?"

"I finally found a barre class I can get to after drop-off—you should come with me!") but we also encourage each other to do better. One of my favorite yoga instructors always says the best way to convince someone to live a happier and healthier life is to do it yourself. Over time, people will want what you have and start asking you questions! I think moms operate that way with one another. You see a mom who looks good, smiles a lot, seems content, you ask questions. She offers her wisdom. Maybe she invites you to come along to her favorite fitness or wellness activity. That's how it works. How do you think giant countrywide walks like the Avon breast cancer walk have been so successful? We inspire one another toward good and we desperately need that inspiration, especially in the thick of motherhood.

Why Building a Community Is an Essential Step to Entrepreneurship

Just as an excess of self-reliance can lead to Mommy burnout, an excess of self-reliance can ware down the founder of any small business or charitable organization, before it's even off the ground! Birthing an idea takes as much bravery as birthing a child. Sure, you could do both alone in the woods—but why would you want to? We need one another and here are a few reasons why:

No one can do it alone

There are a million details associated with creating anything. How could we possibly know what it takes to build a website, host an event, hire an accountant? We need the wisdom and expertise of the people around us to put us in motion. I'm speaking from a very practical angle here—we need people who know more than we do to get us off the ground. We live in a day and age when YouTube can teach us how to do just about anything, but I still prefer a conversation with someone who has actually built a business from scratch. As you brainstorm your ideas, keep a running list of all your questions, perhaps categorizing them so they stay organized. When you meet a knowledgeable person, you will be ready to dialogue in a meaningful way. When I had the idea of creating the *Beyond Mom* community, you bet I had many coffee dates with women who had paved the path of building communities, both online and offline, and had created businesses that revolved around inspiring women. I got great ideas, as well as incredibly tangible resources that helped to push my efforts along. As I imagine my efforts without these conversations and connections, not only would the process have been much less exciting, but everything I learned saved me significant *time*. And for moms, time is *everything*.

We need to know what's possible

It's hard to keep your head up day in and day out. Starting something of your own requires an immense amount of confidence and positivity. I don't know about anyone else, but I don't always have an endless supply of all that good stuff. There are two things I rely on: the inspiration of women who have done it themselves (*if she did it, then maybe I can!*) and the encouragement of the women who believe in me (*what you're doing is amazing and makes such an impact—thank you!*). It's not that our ego needs stroking per se, more that our effort and passion need recognition. We need other people to remind us that the whole darn thing is possible—and worth the inevitable setbacks along the way.

Women are going to help other women

In the community of women building something, I see less competition and more collaboration. I experience a willingness to share ideas, resources, and assistance. Other women aren't seen as competition, but as possible collaborative partners, as a mode to connect with even more of an audience in a way that benefits everyone. Is this a new wave in feminism? I hope so. One of the main reasons I founded *Beyond*

Mom was that I felt there needed to be a collaborative community in which every woman deeply understood what it meant to be a mother *and* a builder. We can't be judged for our realities. Instead, we need to be commended for our accomplishments and the creative ways we get them done. When I have a meeting scheduled with another mom, I'm not angry when I get an email from her that morning that her child is home with pink eye and she must reschedule—*I get it*. I know that if we continue to lean in toward one another, what we can create is so much bigger. Let's accept and encourage this wave of mutual support unique to women and mothers. What we can share is so very powerful.

"You have to find a tribe of women you feel you can relate to. You also have to feel like they're there for you. They've got your back. If somebody's got a fever, they're going to show up and help out, or drop something off, or have your kid over for a sleepover if your husband breaks his foot. Whatever it is, you need to seek those people who can not just support you, but you also trust to support you as a parent by supporting and caring about your child. There is no better feeling than that. I think that is what all moms are looking for."

—**Wednesday Martin, PhD, anthropologist, and author of *The Primates of Park Avenue***

But How Do I Do It?

So now that I've convinced you that you need a community, as both a mother and an entrepreneur in the making, where do you find these incredibly inspiring women who will make it all possible? You might feel like your current crew doesn't fit your new and evolving desires and *that's okay*. It might be tough, but it's a beautiful thing to make new friends and connections based on who you are in the now. Here are some of the things that have helped me . . .

Push yourself past what you think your community is

Though you might identify yourself as a UX designer with a passion for gluten-free cooking, does that mean you might only frequent events for designers or foodies? No! Go past the obvious and meet new people in unexpected ways. Perhaps you attend events that involve a charity you support, or you accept an invitation to a play date in a neighborhood you don't generally venture to. We have to get creative with where we find new and interesting people. For me, I don't frequent only events in the "mom-sphere"—I've found that I run into the same people again and again. I also enjoy attending events in fitness, philanthropy, and healthy eating. I always meet great women who inspire me in entirely unexpected ways.

Get out of the house

This sounds obvious, but as a Mom, it's bizarre how days can go by in the same pair of sweats without a proper shower. Not the best strategy for networking. I'm a big believer in comfort, but also insistent on style. Both are possible, believe me. Dress yourself in a way that makes you feel good and for the love of the goddess, step outside . . . with and without your child. Nothing will get accomplished (except for maybe on your Facebook page) holed up in the house. Get out each day even if it's just to get a coffee and chat with the barista. It keeps things flowing socially.

Go where the people are

During my first year of motherhood, I didn't network solo as much as I did during year two. Between nursing, lack of sleep, and the desire to be with our little ones, of course, we spend more time at home. But once our kids pass the very tiny phase, we can certainly bring them out and enjoy the parenting community with them. You will be surprised by how many interesting women lurk behind the Baby Bjorns and Bugaboos. I remember my son's first summer and the time we spent on a blanket in the park. We met kids of all ages, and I met some of the coolest moms I'd ever met—women who were recovered lawyers and starting clothing swap events, leaving finance and starting websites to coordinate and book kids classes, or opening myriad online businesses. The innovation was off the charts, and I was floored by it. Don't underestimate the mamas you meet; there's probably more going on beneath the surface. So get yourself to the local park, library, or baby music class—your kid will learn the beauty of community and yours will continue to grow.

Online community

As the founder of an online community, it would be weird of me not to mention the power (and immense benefits) of finding community online. I have found Facebook and Instagram hugely beneficial, not only for building the *Beyond Mom* community, but also for meeting other moms whose interests are similar to my own. It's not online dating anymore, but it's certainly online connecting. There are literally websites and community pages for women who want to know one another both as mothers and however else they identify (bloggers, entrepreneurs, networkers, etc.). If you go online, your world can only open more. Just make sure you step outside your front door, too.

Get innovative

What if what you want doesn't exist? Consider creating it. That's what I did. I was frustrated that moms who were also creating a business or a concept and wanted to dialogue on things other than their kids, didn't have a place to connect. *Beyond Mom* was born! It doesn't have to be the biggest of efforts, but perhaps just enough to take you out of your predictable comfort zone. Sometimes what we want doesn't exist yet. So get off your tush and make it happen.

Be the host

It's lovely to attend something that someone else is planning, but every meaningful event needs a good host! Initiate the kiddie picnic in the park or the wine and cheese for new moms (no kids allowed). Ask every woman you know to invite one new person or family. Don't be afraid to lead the way—everyone will be so glad you did and you will get the community experience you've been craving.

Extend yourself

It's a funny dance that new-ish moms do. We can be at the playground, the only two in the park, and no one will say a word. Break the silence! Say hello, introduce the kids, and nine times out of ten, conversation flows from there! Don't be afraid to extend your own warmth and desire for connection. Most other moms seek that same dialogue, but just might be a bit too shy (or exhausted) to speak up.

Initiate

Initiation indicates the ability to create something from nothing, to get something moving in the direction of one's vision. *Beyond Mom's* first event was a circle of "Mompreneurs" standing in my living room, announcing who they were, what they were creating, and what help they needed. I served sandwiches and iced tea. And that day confirmed there was a need for this level of conversation and support. A simple initiation can change the course of not only your own life, but also the women who you are yet to meet. Embrace your ideas, lead with confidence, and don't be afraid to be the voice of your community. Gathering five women and their babies for tea and play is just as valid as building a website for Mompreneurs. At a core level, both provide connection, information, and a sense that we are not alone. And in this world full of millions of mommies and dream builders, we should never ever feel alone.

"Let's first quickly break down why we fear change. We fear change because we have people that we love and places that we love or homes that we love. The fear is that we will lose something. When we say we have a fear of change, that's true, and the reality is when things change, you do lose something. You lose the way it was.

"When your kids are toddlers, that's a sweet time. When they're in middle school, there's a different sweetness, but you must say goodbye to the toddler to get the middle schooler, to get the teenager, to get the young adult, and every single one of those phases of your life is a change.

There's a fear I see with my clients, that if they become successful, what if they're suddenly more successful than their spouse? What happens then?"

—Terri Cole, licensed psychotherapist,
relationship expert, and founder of
The Real Love Revolution.

CHAPTER 5

The Evolving You

Things are Not the Same and I'm Freaking Out!

WE'VE SPENT SOME TIME TALKING ABOUT everyone else—for this conversation let's refer to them as the *external relationships* in our life. But now it's time to get into the nitty-gritty, meaty, deeper conversation, and that's the new relationship we must navigate with ourselves. Why can it be so challenging to reacquaint with the woman who is now a mom? The most simple explanation is that everything has changed. Your body, your thinking, time you have to spend on yourself and, frankly, your entire perception of what it means to be "accomplished" has changed. In the early days, a shower is an accomplishment, where, at one point, negotiating a deal in the corporate world may have been your definition. All these shifts can be overwhelming, and I admit I had a hard time with my new self, which is why this subject is particularly dear to my heart. I had real issues with the layer of belly fat that hung on for months, and felt perplexed as to why certain friendships didn't seem to click anymore. I was always rushing, but, to be frank, I wasn't rushing for sex. Let's just say this was not how I would've defined myself or my life prior to my child arriving on the planet.

So how did I get through it? The answer is simple. But implementing it is one of the hardest things I've ever done. The answer is that you have to *let go of how things were in the past* and accept that *change is the name of the game.* Let me say it in another way. You may have had the tightest abs, an astounding sexual appetite, and a posse of friends reminiscent of *Sex and the City,* but this moment is different than that. Can you accept that without judgment and self-criticism?

This is not something to be glossed over. This is really a vital part of the process. Understand that, if you cannot accept that things have changed and that it is okay, *new you* will have a hard time blossoming because you will always be longing for *old you.*

"I do think that periods of uncertainty are extremely important to embrace. The one thing that's consistent about motherhood is that there is no certainty. There's nothing you can really grasp onto forever, not even the love of your life, your child. You have to expect that they're going to change and evolve. That's been the greatest lesson about mother-hood, that everything is uncertain, and rather than try to control it all and figure out exactly what's happening, let me just be in this period of uncertainty for a while, and be okay with that and ride it out until I either just need to pay the bills or until something emerges out of me."

—Stephanie Sy, news anchor

And we want new you to blossom! She is evolving and she is quite the intriguing character. When I finally accepted that things were different, it allowed me to bask in the freedom, in the possibility surrounding the process that is change. It allowed me to ask questions about how I want my life to look moving forward and I realized, shockingly, that I had clung to certain aspects of my life that weren't totally what I wanted in the first place. Call me a "creative spirit" or call me a Libra—I never knew how to *connect* all the things I loved to do. I loved being a yoga instructor, I loved the media world, strategic problem solving, and I loved being a mama. As I began to accept that life looked different and wouldn't operate exactly how it had before, I began to accept that the things I loved were real parts of me, not just some passing phase. I also started to understand that I wanted both productivity and flexibility. I knew I didn't want to work for anyone else and that I was no longer afraid to launch something. Owning these facts about myself nurtured the fertile ground for *Beyond Mom* to be seeded and flourish.

Right now I'm going to focus on the top five categories of our life that indisputably take the brunt of change post-baby. This is a journey and a process, but it begins with a mindset. One that is accepting, present, and of course, motivated to live the best life possible.

Friendships

As women, we deeply treasure our friendships. We need our sisterhood and, I think, many of our more youthful friendships keep us closer to the cool, upbeat, fun-loving version of ourselves. But, let's face it, things change. The new and evolving you may crave different conversations that aren't rooted in the past. She may crave discussion with women who are seeking more in their lives. Though it's amazing to have friendships with fellow moms, I want to be clear that the friendships that really work for the new you DO NOT have to be with fellow moms! Some of my most meaningful friendships are with women who are at distinctly different phases of their lives, but the level of our connection is deep and potent, so it works. For me, I thrive on having a diverse collection of friends, some moms, some single, some working, some taking a break from working. I enjoy a multitude of conversations and find that they keep me open and alert. What I must have, I've realized, are connections with people that are meaningful, thoughtful, and that speak to this new me on a deeper level.

So, what is required to accept that friendships change and to embrace what or who comes next? There is a certain degree of mourning that is necessary. It's not that there is even a formal breakup, more that some-where in your heart you accept that there is change, and that change can feel sad. Give those feelings time and space. Tears are okay. Generally, if you give *any* emotion some time to breathe, it releases quicker and it can feel easier to move forward. One of my first friendships from college has been one of the hardest to let go of. It's not that anything "happened," more that gradually we didn't have as much in common. What was hard at first was that I felt my being a mom was taking the blame. When really, we were living very different lives. And, our worldviews matched less than they used to. Which was normal for two women who had arrived into their thirties and been friends since they were seventeen. I accepted that I would always love her and if she ever called me I would pick up the phone in a heartbeat. But it was okay if we weren't making the effort right now. That didn't make me a mom failure in the friend department. It actually made me more available for the friendships that felt right in the present. It wasn't easy and sometimes still stings a little, but this is the kind of space clearing that becomes necessary.

What comes next? How do we make connections with friendships that resonate with the "me" now? I notice that if I let my instincts guide me, I end up connecting with new people in a way that feels just right. An example: if I feel a connection to a certain woman in a playgroup, I pursue her for a little extra conversation to see if we really do click. I often seek friendships with people who I meet doing things I enjoy—we immediately know we have something in common. I pay attention to the Me now and who she is drawn to, and I let it unfold. Great spiritual teachers tell us that the hardest work is resisting the natural evolution of our life. In this case, pay attention to what is feeling awkward and what is flowing naturally. The truth will reveal itself from there.

"We navigate through this wild ride of being a mom together; we laugh, cry, panic, prevail, and enjoy this incredible experience that is often surprising and always rewarding.

"Yoga, long walks, birthday parties, pick up and drop off, lunches on those days when I can't find the time or energy to put myself together, you're there. We understand each other in a way that our other friends don't, because our children are also friends, and because we are experiencing together a unique and special time and place in our lives that will never be replaced and will forever be imprinted in our memories.

"I confess, I refer to you as my 'mom friend' but please know that you are so much more . . . you are my *Beyond Mom* friend; an amazing mother that I respect, a friend that I adore, and an irreplaceable and important part of my life."

—**Azizah Rowen, writer, actress, musician, and mom of two**

Body

This subject probably gets the most press. Newsflash: our bodies change after we have babies. But even if we intellectually know to expect it, it can still be a shock when it's *your* body that has changed. Our breasts often lose a bit of tissue after nursing and some of us get stretch marks. At least for a while, it's hard to find our abdominals. Once again, this was a tough pill for me to swallow. As a yogi and a dancer since childhood, let's just say I was "attached" to my body as it was. The first few months after my son was born, I confess I had a few emotional

> "Your body may feel like new terrain, with a changed landscape and new sensations. Give yourself, and your partner, time to explore what's true now. And take heart in the fact that pleasure is every woman's right, and that the more connected and in love you are with your own body, the better mother you'll be."
>
> —**Alexandra Jamieson, Author of *Women, Food, and Desire*, Co-Creator of Super Size Me, and host of Her Rules Radio**

breakdowns when I couldn't fit into my old jeans—or even my maternity jeans! I ended up having to buy jeans that fit me for the moment, but probably wouldn't be something I'd want to put back on in the future. It sucked that I wanted to work out, but I was so incredibly tired. I felt incredibly unsettled and had a few tantrums over it.

Until one day when I took a deep breath and realized that I'd had enough of my own negative talk. I had the power to step into the next phase with my body and though I didn't know what it would look like or how much *success* I would have, I had to start somewhere. So instead of buying jeans, I bought some fresh workout clothes and looked for something to inspire me. It was then that I found spinning. Soul Cycle invited me in with a friendly staff that assured me I could do it. Classes with thumping, inspiring beats helped me forget how tired I felt. I will never forget my first class and how proud I felt that I had made it through—I was capable of far more than I believed. And so began my introduction to the fitness world, to pushing my limits and watching how my body responded.

And then, something incredible happened. Despite nursing, weight gain, and the aches and pains of new motherhood, I found a completely new relationship to my body, one in which I identified as strong versus flexible. I found that strong spoke to what I needed more than ever. People say I hit the "best shape of my life" during that year. What was definitely true was how much I wanted to keep exploring my capabilities. What I will say for sure is that I would never have reached this place had I not accepted that things had changed and I had an opportunity to be surprised. It takes hard work, mentally and physically, but with acceptance and persistence, your potential is limitless.

Time

This one might get second prize in the most sought-after-thing-lost-since-becoming-moms competition. It can seem since the arrival of our little one that after laundry, dishes, food preparation, diaper changing, and scrounging up some energy for our partners, there is scarcely a moment for ourselves, let alone time to actually think about what matters to us on a deeper level. If only we had more time, we lament. *If only, if only, if only.* I believe that the lamenting in this category is conceivably our biggest hurdle. In this case, we really can't get time back. The only option we have is to manage it differently and with care, especially if we suspect we might have an idea to bake. So take a moment my friends, take a deep breath and tell yourself: *there are only twenty-four hours in a day. Some of those hours I need to sleep. During my waking hours, I must manage my mom life and my desire to cultivate myself as an individual. I need not freak out. I merely need to set my goals and manage my time in a realistic way, given my new circumstances.*

Unfortunately, many of the women who come to me for help have fallen into one of two traps: either they are so hung up on how little time they have that they do nothing, otherwise known as *paralysis*; or they have not accepted that time functions differently now and have completely overburdened themselves to the point of deep exhaustion, otherwise known as *burnout*. Is there a middle ground?

I believe that, as moms, we do need to accept that time is not our own *in the same way*. But the time we do define as our own can be used very wisely and efficiently.

> ## *A CEO of a major men's magazine once said that he always wants a mom to be part of his team—she is always the most organized and efficient player.*

It's clear that we must adapt to time as it is in the present and find the best way to work with it. Give me three hours to get a chapter written, an email drafted, and hit a spin class? I'll get it done. Necessity is the mother of invention and time management becomes an imperative skill as a *Beyond Mom*. So, let go of resisting the fact that it's changed and begin to ponder how to work constructively and realistically with what you've got.

I've learned a lot about modern-day busyness from my friend Hope, a life coach and mom. When most people ask you how you are, do you answer with the word "busy?" I do. I'm trying to shift that through my own awareness and my own understanding of time. Can we get off the attachment to perfection and instead slow down and give ourselves the gift of quiet, simple moments, without our technology attached to us? We live in a plugged in world and it makes us feel like we have no break. Hope reminds us that we really do have a choice *not* to participate in the busy story we tell ourselves and others. How can you give yourself the gift of unplugged, quiet space? Trust me, a little goes a long way.

"We cannot make more time. It's not so much about needing more time. It's about making mindful choices with what we're doing with it. Especially women who have young kids, you're in a very busy phase of life. Don't tell yourself the story that this is inevitably crazy because as soon as you tell yourself the story that it is, like, 'Oh, life is crazy. I'm whirling around,' you're going to look for evidence to support that. Refuse to participate in that story. Instead say, 'There is enough space for everything I want to do,' and I think you can find evidence of that as well."
—Laura Vanderkam, author of *I Know How She Does It: How Successful Women Make the Most of Their Time*

Sex

As you recall in some of my prior personal revelations, sex was a complicated and emotional category for me in the months following my son's birth and it is for many of us. We both want it and don't want it. Need it and can't find the time for it. Think about it but feel too tired to do it. Sex seems to enter a very conflicted territory once we have a child (or multiple children). Even if we finally break past the anxiety of the first few encounters after birth (and rejoice in the fact that we're not physically broken—our parts still work!), we still collide with the fact that our *relationship* to sex is different. There are always exceptions to the rule, but most of us don't relate to our sexual life in the same way after we've had a baby. Our desire or appetite for it might be different for some time. Our body might respond to sensation differently. We may feel like we have no physical energy for it, yet emotionally wish we did.

"We underestimate how many hours we sleep. It makes sense. We overestimate the things we don't want to do and we underestimate the things we want to do. That's human nature. It feels like it takes less time if you love to do it, and so because of this, we tend not to see where available time might be. We tell ourselves the same story, 'I have no time.' Hence, when free time does appear, you don't know what you want to do with it because you're telling yourself you have no time.

"You tend to spend it in the most obvious, non-chosen ways, like surfing the web, pattering around the house, watching TV. Those are fine in small doses but they tend not to be the things that people find most meaningful or enjoyable. Knowing that the time might be there helps you make better choices about where you want the time to go.

"What if you just stare at the sky, stare at the clouds? This is time that could be completely slow moving, indolent, wonderful, and sometimes instead, you find yourself reading an article or scrolling newsfeeds you don't actually care about. I think the idea is that we want to spend less time speeding time up because that's what a lot of us do, filling up spaces of boredom, but you don't have to. If you feel like you have no time, look at what you're doing at night from 8:30 to 10:30 p.m.

"Sometimes people are working during that time slot, but often they are just watching TV or surfing the web. Don't do that. Go outside, sit on the porch, watch the sunset, watch the stars come out. Those two hours, if you don't have your phone in hand, are going to seem like an incredibly long period of time, a very slow-moving, hopefully relaxing, but at least very slow-moving two hours. That's available to people most nights but we just choose not to do it."

—**Laura Vanderkam, author of** *I Know How She Does It: How Successful Women Make the Most of Their Time*

Remember everything you've been through over the past year or two? In this section, I'd like to encourage you to move toward a new place of peace in regards to sex. Remember, if you can accept that something is now different, you open up the door for something *even better* to show up. If you resist change, you smother the opportunity for growth. Can you approach this part of your life with less judgment and more compassion?

Here's a little more of my personal experience—like many of us, I judged the fact that my sex life was different than it was before. I worried that we would never find the time to connect again, I allowed emotions and worry about the fate of my marriage to get the better of me. I eventually realized that I was telling myself stories I manufactured out of fear. My marriage was intact, as was my sexual self. I just needed to give room for the changes that had happened and allow everything to catch up. And not surprisingly, my husband wasn't worried at all! He understood that we were merely adjusting to a new phase in our lives. What evolved was surprising and taught me a lot about what can happen when you stop telling yourself fear-based stories and allow time to take care of you.

As sex crept back into the picture, I realized that the sexual connection with my husband felt very mature. And that does not mean it was boring. It means it was anchored in real love and real connection based on the life we were co-creating, and I really felt that expressing itself. As my body healed and got stronger, I also noticed a sense of body awareness and confidence I didn't have before. Even though birth can make you feel weak in the beginning, the fact that you have brought another human onto the planet is not only gratifying, but also awe-inspiring. No man can do it, and so only our deep and most primal femininity is responsible for such a miraculous thing. And that's kind of sexy. Over time, I experienced an interesting fact: the more confident I became in myself as a woman, a creator, a thinker . . . the more pleasure I was able to achieve in my sexual moments. Is this what they call a "sexual prime?" Perhaps. With time, I begin to realize that a sexual prime is likely a deeper connection to self and thus, more sexual abandon and pleasure.

I find this evolution to be fascinating and through plenty of conversations with *Beyond Moms* (often accompanying a glass of wine), I discovered I'm not the only one. With age comes more confidence and a more clear relationship to the sexual person we are. So even if you feel you are in a "funk" post-baby, understand that with conscious navigation and self-growth, there is a world yet to unfold for you. But you must make peace with the phases as they arise and understand that they are part of the evolving you finding its new normal.

Self-Care

As moms, we dream of massages, manicures, and quiet cups of tea. We do so much giving that we yearn for someone and something to give back to us. I remember trying on clothing in a store one day, my son was only nine months old, and the lady helping me was particularly sweet. She helped pull a top over my head and so gently fixed the top and my hair, her fingers like a gentle breeze. I couldn't believe how lovely her touch felt; I was almost brought to tears. I realized in that moment how much dressing, fixing, and nurturing I did on a daily basis for my little guy and how completely nourishing it felt for someone to simply arrange my hair.

It's so tempting when we're trying to address the above time issue to knock self-care off the table as a way to make room for other things. But we are the engine that drives the family car! So while society might tell us that we should be able to do it all, let's recognize that in order to be able to give as much as we do we *must* give back to ourselves. I argue it's an equation of balance. The more you give, the more you need to take.

So getting back to our foundational concept: first we must accept that there's something different. In this case, we are giving on autopilot. It never stops. We may start to notice our energy dwindling or that we cry when a sales lady helps us in the dressing room (like I did). Our realization may be that there's something else we need to begin feeling more balanced, more energized, more fueled. Begin to ask yourself what would make you feel more full? Is it a good book and the time to read it?

A bubble bath once a week? Or a once-a-month professional massage? There are so many chains across the country that offer memberships now. A closet cleanse? (My friend Jenny is a stylist who specializes in closet cleanses, particularly for new moms. WOW. It was a life altering experience, and I would definitely put it in the category of self-care— you begin to see your entire style self differently, so a closet cleanse and some new items begin to help the evolving you show up fully. If you can't afford a stylist, bring your best friend in and do the work together!) What can you afford to give yourself both in terms of time and money? My experience is that the biggest hurdle is giving yourself permission. I am grabbing you by the shoulders right now and telling you this is not self-indulgence, this is vital self-care. The second biggest hurdle is time. This is where, Miss *Beyond Mom*, you must get creative. Can you find another mom who also needs some self-love and perhaps you swap kids two times a month? First slot goes to mama one to get a manicure and pedicure, second slot goes for a yoga class and the time for a bubble bath for mama two. If you accept that you *need* it, you can begin to create the conditions for getting it. Ready, set, go.

Standard of Work Output

Prior to having children, most of us work at our own pace and at our own time. Even if we work for someone else, our output is based on what's going on with our individual selves. Ask any mom how quickly her agenda changes the minute her child wakes up with hives or an earache. Ask her how easy it is to draft an email when her two-year-old is clawing at her leg to watch "Daniel Tiger's Neighborhood" on her computer *again*. Our ability to put forth our work becomes compromised and that alone is a major adjustment. Many *Beyond Moms* were high performers in their chosen fields and find the concept of putting anything out there that is less than perfect absolutely abominable. Insert child? Well, it's a rude awakening. We can't always produce at our "normal" output, in the timing we would want it and with the focus we might crave.

Let's go back to our process. First we'll state the facts. In this case: our work output is challenged now that we're moms and we often find it very difficult, if not impossible, to produce to the level that we would've once expected of ourselves. Take a deep breath. Because we must rewire our thinking. I recently chatted with a mom I know after a spin class who admitted she had put her accessory business aside because she couldn't find consecutive time to get anything done. I encouraged her to just think about things differently. If what she felt she needed was consecutive time to work, perhaps she should change the hours she hired her babysitter from three mornings a week to two full days.

Another woman I know, a highly successful style blogger, found herself sucked into the vortex of her two small children in her apartment, even once her nanny arrived. After numerous discussions about her workflow and budget, we determined that having an office space is what would get her out of the house and keep her productive. An office wasn't what she originally anticipated needing. Many bloggers tend to work from home, enjoying that they can produce anywhere. But this woman was no ordinary woman—she was a mother! What she needed to produce her work shifted and she had to get with the times. She quickly found a space near her home and noticed instantaneously how focused she became there, as well as how much more easily she left the house in the morning. She had somewhere to go and so . . . go she must. At the end of the day (which was sometimes three o'clock in the afternoon if she felt like it), she returned home feeling productive and satisfied. We have to be nimble with our needs, willing to create new pathways of productivity, not based on how things *used* to be, but based on our current challenges. Remember we are not producing as the single woman with no reason to rush home. We have very concrete windows of time where we must get it all done. So figure out the way to accomplish your best based on your current situation. Get real, get creative, and recognize that with the right support, the world is still very much your oyster.

"You know, it's funny, I used to only write in the mornings. And that was sacred for me before I had a child—early morning time was my writing time. I felt most alert. I felt most in touch with the muse. You roll out of bed and you go straight into this creative space. I never booked meetings before 10:00 or 11:00 a.m. And I would wake up at 6:00 a.m. so I had that really quiet, amazing time. My husband is not a morning person, so our whole house would be quiet. I did not believe that I could write good, creative work at other parts of the day.

"I had a day several months ago that was just so pivotal for me because it was one which I had blocked off the whole day for writing. It had been yet another night when sleep didn't go as expected. So I had been up most of the night. When our nanny arrived, I needed to go to sleep for most of the morning, if I was going to function at all. So there I was, I woke up at 1:00 p.m. and I had a forty-five-minute block of time. And my heart just wanted to write. It had been a writing day on my calendar, and I had missed it. So it was a huge moment when I said to myself, 'We have from 2:00 until 2:45 p.m., and this essay is going to get written right now. Let's see if my brain can adapt.'

"And I wrote it. By 2:45, I was on such a high because I had written. And I love writing. I was actually quite surprised that I could do it in forty-five minutes, instead of three hours. And I could do it in the afternoon. So there's this sense of losing the preciousness about amounts of time, routines, and the perfectionism. Being willing to continue to create, and read, and do our work in a very foggy, imperfect, constantly changing space. That has been a lot of what accepting change is all about."

—Tara Mohr, women's leadership and well-being expert, author of *Playing Big, Practical Wisdom for Women Who Want To Speak Up, Create and Lead*

"I'm committed to trying my best. I am always handing it over to the universe. In hard moments, I ask, 'is there a better way for me to be doing this?' If so, show me the way. And the beautiful thing is, I always receive some form of intuition or guidance. It might not happen right away—I usually have to calm down a bit before I can really hear it. It can be easy to get caught in the murky, anxiety-ridden waters of new parenthood. I know I have had plenty of moments, especially in those first few months when so much doubt comes up. But by turning it over to a higher power or love or the universe, whatever you want to call it, helps me know that I am being guided along this parenting journey, and that I am capable of the job and that my husband and I are not alone in the responsibility."

—Christina Justiz Roush, mother,
founder of Brooklyn Baby Bumps,
and co-founder of Girl Gift Gather

CHAPTER 6

Moving Past the Doubt

"Unlike a lot of other people in the women's empowerment world, I'm not a fan of the argument that women should become more confident. I don't think that's actionable advice for us. But I do think we can learn how to have a different relationship to our self-doubt. Accepting that it's always going to be there, but not taking direction from it. Taking direction from our aspirations, our vision, and our desires for our life."

—Tara Mohr, women's leadership and well-being expert, and author of *Playing Big: Practical Wisdom for Women Who Want to Speak Up, Create, and Lead*

So, You're Ready to Build Something . . .

YOU'VE DONE THE WORK. YOU'VE CONNECTED to your body, your mind, and your community. You've gotten your relationships in order. You are the fertile ground to create something powerful for yourself and to offer society. Congratulations! Isn't it fascinating, however, how quickly we can freeze the moment we tell ourselves we're READY? A whole slew of other issues and anxieties arise the minute we have an idea and determine that the moment is *now*. But never fear, my dear, *Beyond Mom* is here. Through a sometimes slow and painful process of my own, and hundreds of conversations with women at the seed phase of their business ideas, I've uncovered a few important and timeless truths that might help you feel more "normal" about your fears and more "prepared" for your process. Part II of this book will take this solid personal foundation you've built, insights from some of the most action-oriented businesswomen I know, and guide you toward a launch of your idea. But before we continue, on let's acknowledge a few more concerns.

You've Got the Feeling for It but You're Not 100 Percent Sure What IT Is

I'm the perfect example of someone who had a calling, but not a clue. I was a yoga teacher for years, and when I got pregnant, I wanted to create a space where I could write many of the stories and ideas I'd shared with my yoga students. I created a blog, which I now realize (years later) was "Beyond Mom 1.0." What I knew was that I wanted to inspire women, I wanted to speak openly and honestly, but I wasn't sure the precise form it would all take. So I gave myself some time to write and let motherhood wash over me. When my son was just shy of a year old, I began leading yoga retreats for moms to give back to themselves and gained tremendous insight by simply talking to the many women I met at these retreats. I started to understand a missing pocket in the market—a community for moms who wanted to develop their sense of self within the motherhood experience. I began to recognize a market for such a concept. And a solid year after my blog launched and I invested some time and money into it, I began to understand what IT really was. Sometimes it isn't linear. But I find that if you're actively paying attention and engaging with your process, the answers will flow freely. Make yourself available for it with a sense of both patience and persistence.

What Did You Love about What You Did Before?

Building something up from the ground can be liberating—and also scary. You're unsure where to put your energies and focus. This is the perfect and opportune time to reflect upon what your favorite parts of your prior professional career were. Most entrepreneurs will tell you that the early days require an all-hands-on-deck attitude and if you are starting out solo, it's likely you're going to find yourself doing everything. You're going to be the marketing department, IT, and payroll. While this is completely normal at the beginning, you don't want it to be that way forever and the best way to ensure that it isn't—and that you'll be staffing up the right positions when you grow—is to ask yourself exactly what part of a venture gives you pleasure. Where do you want this business to go and what role do you want to have in it as it grows? Important questions you must ask yourself:

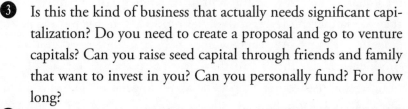

1. What did you love doing most in your prior positions? Did you love diving into tasks that required immense organization and focus—or did you thrive during strategy meetings and building new key relationships?

2. Are you comfortable functioning as the sole entrepreneur in this budding business? In other words, are you comfortable living with some risk and investing a bit of money into your idea? Or do you feel that you would function better with a partner to hold some of the stress alongside you?

3. Is this the kind of business that actually needs significant capitalization? Do you need to create a proposal and go to venture capitals? Can you raise seed capital through friends and family that want to invest in you? Can you personally fund? For how long?

4. Do you like to make the decisions or do you enjoy truly collaborating with another equal to design a vision? Maybe you should form a partnership.

These are the kinds of questions that you simply must ask yourself from the conception of your idea. You must dialogue with them even more now that you have reached the "ready" stage—it's so very easy to create your own company and find that you're spending the majority of your time sorting through your contacts—or dealing with invoicing—when you really want to be out networking. This is the information that will allow you to create a vision of the team that will support you and, most importantly, help you create a company that brings you joy.

Why? Because you'll actually be doing what you love.

Don't hesitate . . . GO!

One of my greatest challenges as a perfectionist is pressing the "Go" button. It's so easy to tell yourself that your product or idea just isn't ready for the world to know about. I'm famous for telling myself that I will promote something just as soon as I (fill in the blank with almost anything). As much as I'm a believer in properly branding yourself to achieve a professional look and feel, I'm an even bigger believer in getting out there and talking about what you're passionate about. I love when women come to my events to share the news of what's coming soon. It shows that they have the confidence in what they're creating. Unequivocally, the women who have attended my mixers and passionately shared their ideas without limiting language or downplaying what they are launching (even if the final product is not yet available) have launched with a bang. These women believe in the *process*, not only the product, and are thrilled to share it even during its infancy. I've also noticed that the women who aren't afraid to get out there and get moving understand and embody that in the end: *YOU ARE THE MOST VALUABLE PLAYER.* Yes, despite all anxiety and all details, you are the most important piece of the puzzle because you are the visionary. If you have the passion behind your endeavor, then you are ready to get out there, talk about it, and start making it happen. Because the reality is that you're going to learn from both your successes and your mistakes, and the only way to begin that learning is to get going. Failure is part of the process and not something to fear. Every small letdown is just information that helps to shape the next steps taken. So hesitate not. Take a deep breath and get out there. Who's the MVP? You are!

And now as you turn the page toward Part II, know that you are about to receive some very specific guidance not just from me but from women who have walked the walk and talked the talk, who have decades of experience and are sharing it with you, from the women I personally speak to when I have questions about my time, business development, branding, and more. How lucky are we?!

You might not discover all the answers necessary for your specific concept, but you will receive a metaphorical flashlight that will shine a light on your early idea footprints and the steps to take to turn it into a reality. If you begin to feel overwhelmed, slow down and trust that you have built a strong and stable foundation inside and outside of your home, in your community, your family, and within your body and mind. That is a huge start and a valuable launching pad.

And most importantly, trust that you have the tools, the intelligence, and the ingenuity to create something special . . . but of course you do! After all, you are a mom!

"You've spent countless hours churning, building, and planning out your idea, now is the moment of truth; it's ready to be released into the world. Gulp—anxiety sets, you tense up and freeze. 'What if it all goes wrong? What if I missed something? What if no one shows up?' These thoughts or some version of them will undoubtedly creep up the moment it's time to pull the trigger on your idea. When this happens, the most important thing to remember is: this is normal. Just because you're feeling anxious about your idea or even a bit panicked, is not an indication that something's wrong. So when those feelings pop up, welcome them and don't hide behind them. They are part of the creative process. Being at the cusp of turning your idea into a reality is a tall feat—don't do it alone, enlist help. Call on your support system, whether that is your partner, a colleague, a coach, or your best friend. Their job is to be there with you and stand alongside you when your legs feel a bit wobbly.

Immediately after your launch or soon after, it's a good idea to step away from it. Put some space in between the results of your hard work and your next step. This separation gives you an opportunity to clear your mind, detach a bit, so you can refocus your energies and keep moving forward confidently. A client of mine after years of writing her book, caught the anxiety bug in the days leading up to its launch. While helping her acknowledge that her nerves were normal so she could manage them better, she was able to move through it more calmly and even took herself on a day trip to unplug before embarking on her book tour. Anything worth doing will bring up anxiety, so with a calm mind and help by your side, you'll tackle it with ease."

**—Ariane Hunter, career coach,
CPC Purposeful Living**

PART II

FROM IDEA TO ACTION

"It's probably safe to call every mom a '*Beyond Mom*,' I love the idea of recognizing that all moms go above and beyond—personally and/or professionally. To me, the only way I could be a mom was to keep doing what I've always done, which is writing for TV and film. We have a picture of me nursing my daughter Thelma while I was sitting at the computer, working on a script that was due weeks after I'd given birth. It wasn't even a choice for me; it was just my life. The same thing happened again when my son Roscoe was born and another script was due, and it's pretty much continued that way ever since! (Minus the nursing, thank God.)"

—Julie Rottenburg, mother, executive producer of Show Runner, and head writer of Odd Mom Out

CHAPTER 7

Conceiving Your Idea

FOR MANY OF US, THERE IS a period of time prior to conception, where we begin to imagine motherhood and what it must be like. We look at squishy cute babies in their stroller, adorable baby outfits in the window, and daddies doting on their stumbling toddlers in the park. We begin to imagine what our version of that might look like. We might start to dream up how our home space might shift as well as how we might shape our work schedule. What would our family dynamic feel like with a new addition? And of course, what will it feel like to love someone the way we love our child? This dreamy stage has a specific function. It creates the fertile space in our lives to welcome a child. Our ovaries and uterus must be fertile, of course, but so must our energy and space. We probably don't even realize how important this period is, but its potent and powerful if we tune in to it.

Heard of manifestation? This dreaming and visioning stage is part of it. It's when our being starts to line up with what we want to attract into our life.

Many *Beyond Moms* are naturally productive individuals, we may as well go as far as to say overachievers. We have an idea and we tend to dive in headfirst. A *Beyond Mom* business is a special kind as it must not only be profitable but must also work with who we are and how we want our life to flow. I argue, therefore, that it takes a little bit more time to strike that balance and to be clear with what we're creating and why.

Contrary to the *let's dive in* philosophy of many entrepreneurs, I urge you to slow down as your ideas begin to marinate and to give them room to breathe. Your business IS your other baby, so begin to dream how you will welcome it into your life. Here are a few practices that might help you become more "idea fertile." Many of these ideas you may recognize from Part I of this book, and that's not a coincidence. We must get closer to our core and our foundation to create ideas of substance.

> "If someone has a stirring, a feeling they want more, they want to do something differently, you've got to get quiet. You've got to become still and silent and be with that feeling, instead of getting into action right away, which is what most effective, efficient women would like to do. We just want the checklist, just tell me what to do. Instead, really allow yourself to be in the not knowing, which may be uncomfortable, but the knowing will come from that place."
>
> **—Terri Cole, licensed psychotherapist, relationship expert, and founder of The Real Love Revolution**

Practices for Idea Fertility

Intentional Breathing

Why am I not calling it meditation? Once baby arrives and you're doing the mom juggle, meditation as a concept can feel a little challenging to carve out time for. So how about reframing it and instead attempt to breathe with more intention while nursing, walking, cooking, showering, slowing down for sleep, etc. You will begin to notice that breathing helps steady your thoughts and ease any anxiety that might come up when inviting a new idea into your life. It's in this space of focus and steadiness that some of our best and realistic thoughts can reveal themselves. So invite more breathing into your life.

Creative Conversations

Remember when you used to hang out with your friends who were already moms and you would listen to them talk about everything from baby sleep patterns, to strollers, to teething, and of course, about how obsessed they are with their new baby. It's not that you could completely understand it, but you were certainly absorbing the energy of love that encompasses motherhood and learning the details as the conversation unfolded. The same goes for creating a fertile environment for your business. Put yourself in the midst of people who are idea builders, creators, and overall positive individuals about their work. Hear about what they are working on, ask questions, absorb their energy and know that it is sinking into you. After you hang with these folks, jot down a few notes of what inspired you the most or what further questions you have. Which leads me to . . .

Take Notes! Ideas are Everywhere

If you see a cool store window that inspires you, or a product that you wish you'd thought of, and most importantly, if you notice something that doesn't exist in the market place but you wish did. Mommy brain is real, as discussed in Part I, so don't lose your ideas. They are precious and worthy of the moment so jot them down!

Let me confess, my worst moments business-wise (and mother-hood-wise) have been when I didn't give an idea its due time. Or when I simply didn't create the conditions for the right idea to evolve. When our great idea arrives into our life, do we want to be erratic, anxiety ridden, and uninspired? I'd guess we'd prefer to be grounded, calm, and surrounded by people excited to support our creative flow.

I remember when I found out I was pregnant with my first child, I was so ready for him to come into my world. I had gone through a miscarriage and rather than spending too much time on the sadness of it, I allowed the experience to guide me closer to my husband and toward the motherhood I wanted. I spent time with friends who had babies whom I admired and listened to the stories my female relatives told me about raising babies. Even though I was a nervous first-time mother, I felt energetically ready for my baby to come into my world.

I'd say the same about my *Beyond Mom* brand. I had been teaching yoga, writing my blog, and chatting with entrepreneurial moms. The stories of my students and the inspiration of businesswomen I knew moved into my body and mind and inspired me toward the lifestyle and business I was eventually ready to create. What was my key? Time.

I truly took my son's first year of life to allow my ideas to unfold. This was indeed a luxury as many women don't have that sort of time, but you can create fertile ground for ideas, no matter what the conditions.

Family Tree Exercise

One of the most elucidating exercises I take my clients through is the Family Tree Exercise. What I want you to write down is, going as far back as you can on both sides, how did people in your family make money? I realized that, even if it was a fruit cart, people in my family had always been entrepreneurs—why should I be different? I bet you'll find themes. Is it service? Teaching? Liking to be part of a larger organization? This will give you clues about how to not only structure your venture but most importantly, even more motivation to embrace your natural born inclination and skills. The apple doesn't fall far from the tree!

Inviting Your Idea in and Making Sure It's the Right One for You

Most business ideas fit into one of four categories: a product-driven business, an online/content business, a non-profit, or a service-based business. For a *Beyond Mom* business to thrive, we must analyze all parts of it not only for feasibility, but also whether it creates the lifestyle we want for our family. It's a more depth-filled analysis, if you will. We will dive into the details of each of these business types in upcoming chapters, but for now let's discuss how you are thinking through this early idea.

I've created a list of questions that supports your personal analysis of any idea, regardless of the category of business it fits into. These questions, if answered, will help you navigate the concepts and ideas as this book unfolds. Most importantly, your answers will help to reveal the experience you want your business to provide you. By the way, these reflective questions and answers you will share are much of the information required for a business plan. Take your time and watch how much information reveals itself to you. It's all inside of *you*; open up to the questions and answers unfolding!

Twenty Questions to Make Sure You're Getting Pregnant with the Right Idea

1. What's the need?
2. Who are you serving?
3. What is your market?
4. How does your idea fit that market?
5. How quickly do you need to monetize?
6. Will you need an investor?
7. Do you have the basics? An up-to-date computer, printer, and phone?
8. Who is doing what you want to do well?

9. Where do you see room for improvement?

10. Which of your skills are applicable to this idea?

11. What parts of this idea do you feel like you will need support for?

12. How will this play to your strengths?

13. What do you love about it?

14. Are there any places where building this business will touch up against your moral framework? Can you align them? For example, this frequently comes into play for my *Beyond Moms* thinking about foreign manufacturing.

15. How is this similar to what you were doing before children? How is it different?

16. How many hours a week do you want to put in?

17. What do you want to be doing five years from now?

18. How old are your kids and what will their needs from you be over that same period?

19. What are you comfortable with missing out on at home?

20. What is non-negotiable?

Spend time with what these questions revealed. Do you notice any themes? Is there any fear dictating your answers? Is there anything you want to work through or heal so your choices are based on confidence and not trepidation? And of course, do you still feel positive about pursuing your budding concept? Does it need to be altered in any way to shift toward your goals?

I'm surrounded by some incredible entrepreneurs who have boiled their early process into some actionable steps—here's a few of those stories, musings, and steps for you. I'm sharing several because I've noticed that different expertise works for me for different reasons and at different times. Be open to various voices and styles that I am providing you. Many of the ideas suggested next will be expanded upon in the sections to come.

Quick tips for a woman with an idea! By Heather MacDowell, founder of Tickle Water

① **Talk about your idea to anybody and everybody you see, encounter, and meet.** I think it's important to get outside feedback. If over and over you keep hearing, "Oh, I don't think that's a good idea," or "This would be a problem," or "What about this?" or "I've seen that already a hundred times." You might be getting all kinds of negative feedback, but you might be getting all kinds of positive. Whatever you're getting, that feedback is going to motivate you one way or another or it's going to give you the information that you need to take the next step.

② **Put it out there to make it more than an idea!** I almost feel like putting it out there to the universe makes it more real in your mind so it's not just an idea. It's actually starting to come to life as you put it out there. Some people say not to share your ideas or someone is going to steal it. It would take a tremendous amount of effort on someone else's part to actually steal your idea and go do it. Most people are too absorbed in their own life to be able take someone else's life. I think it's excellent to put the idea out there and ask questions and get feedback from anybody who wants to give it.

③ **Stay true to yourself.** If you have an idea that you believe in and you think there's something behind it, stay true to yourself and hold onto that confidence knowing you've got something special and you can turn it into something. Success does not happen overnight and I am so far from knowing whether or not even knowing Tickle Water is a success or not, but you just keep plugging forward. Every single day.

Mind Habits and Thought Bits for Entrepreneurial Growth
by Claudia Chan, founder of SHE
Global Media and SHE Summit

1. What is your source?
2. Think of the biggest version of your vision—this is the way you take bigger steps
3. Take your vision seriously—its been cast upon you!
4. Expect the obstacles but know they are there to build you
5. Keep going and build your tribe
6. Build your mind!

Guidelines for Entrepreneurial Women by Jenny Powers:
"Running with Heels wasn't my first business idea, but it was the first time I knew in my gut, I can't live without this. This is what I want to wake up and do. If I won the lottery tomorrow, I would still want to find a way to build a women's community and support working women and mothers. In building my business I've learned the importance of:

1. **Mindset.** One of the things I learned about myself and also from the women I've interviewed is that the number one ingredient for success is mindset. If you don't believe in yourself and you don't believe in your work, it's not going to happen.

    Visualizing your success and working towards manifesting it is really critical. Most of the women I know believed they could do it from the onset. There was no plan B because having a plan B meant that plan A might not work. We didn't want to think about it that way.

2. **Asking for help!** Another thing is asking for help. So many people see asking for help as a sign of weakness, but I really consider it a sign of confidence and strength because you know if you don't ask, you don't get. Everyone thinks you don't need anything because you appear to be holding yourself together and helping others through your specific expertise. But making yourself vulnerable and admitting when you don't know how to do something is key to moving forward. I didn't know anything about technology. I was terrified to launch my podcast. Now I sit with my microphone and I feel like a pro every week.

3. **Collaboration, not competition!** We need to really focus on the mindset of collaboration and not competition. If we can raise up one woman, we can raise up women in general. We should really be supporting and engaging one another throughout."

From here, start to write an idea concept with more concrete language, perhaps taking some of the incredible wisdom above into account. It doesn't have to be perfect or perfectly flushed out, but this will allow you to spend time thinking specifically on your idea concept, to see how the details sit with you. It also allows you to begin garnering support around what was revealed. For example, if you discovered that you will need some child-care support to have enough time to pursue this idea, you can begin doing research or asking friends for suggestions. Or if you need to expand your technology assets, you can take the time now to get the proper computer, phone, or back up system you might need to be productive.

If the concept of collaboration felt totally right to you, how do you build that philosophy into your model and who can you involve in it?

Exploratory Conversations and Networking

Remember how in Part I, I stressed the importance of building a like-minded community? It originally functioned as a support system as you aligned your body and mind with motherhood, but now you will use it to support your budding creation. Now that your idea is a little more concrete and fleshed out, when potential mentors ask you any of the above questions you'll be ready with answers. Always be honest. Say, "I'm thinking about starting X. I admire what you do, and I'd love to take you to coffee to get some advice." You don't have to pretend to be farther along then you are in the process. But, to be taken seriously, you have to know your idea inside and out. The above questions and time you spent organizing and reflecting after you completed them will allow you to speak clearly and effectively when you have these exploratory meetings.

Some quick meeting tips:

1. Have your questions prepared ahead so you don't forget to ask them!

2. Do your research on the person you're meeting with—it's nice to know what they've actually written, businesses they've started, or interviews they've done.

3. Offer to buy them their coffee! This person is being generous with their time; you can buy them coffee.

4. Close every meeting with a quick review of "next steps." Example: *So, I will send you that article I mentioned I read this weekend and you will introduce me to your book club friend who you think I should chat with? Great!*

5. Follow up every chat with a "thank you!" Perfection isn't necessary when you're ideating but manners and gratitude are always in style.

I can assure you that after hosting several years of events for the *Beyond Mom* community, the need for in-person connection and meaningful discussion is real and very much alive.

Their willingness to share information and resources as well as encouragement and good faith has revealed to me the importance of

Women, especially moms with ideas, thrive around one another.

bringing women together in real time. It's important to fine tune your networking skills as Jenny so carefully explained above, but it's also important to find your like-minded folk. As you begin the networking process, seek to find people who show up authentically, who ask as many questions as they do answer them, who give smiles and warmth as much as they do concrete advice. Find places where you can show up as you, the glowing mother and businesswoman that you are. I watch the buzzing excitement of my event attendees as they meet, share ideas, show kid photos, sip champagne, and feed off one another's positive energy. It always inspires me to watch this in action. Where can you find this for yourself? Even if you don't live in New York City where you can attend my regular events (please come if you can though!), I assure you that women want to gather right where you are. Find a way to meet them and connect in real time.

More on networking and its incredible power to jump-start your process!

"Maybe you're returning from maternity leave or perhaps now that your children are grown up, you've decided it's time to re-enter the workforce, whatever the reason may be. Welcome back!

"While it's natural to be anxious and a bit nervous, you're actually in a great place to start over from square one and learn how to network in the most efficient and stress-free way possible. So instead of worrying about your networking skills being a little rusty, think of your re-entry as the perfect opportunity to start fresh with the way you approach meeting people. Most people hate networking because it seems inauthentic and sales-y —but it doesn't have to.

"Rather than thinking of networking as you know it, think about it as the act of meeting people and connecting with them. In essence that's really all networking is. And if we think about it that way we won't feel as much pressure. So when you walk into a big room filled with people milling about wearing nametags, look around and see who you would like to meet and then go and introduce yourself. Don't think about filling a quota, don't think about making a sale, just think of it as getting to know one another. People do business with people they like so before you should even attempt to do business you should focus on being liked. How do you get people to like you? Just by being yourself. Forget the 'dress like the job you want, not the one you have' advice. Forget the 'fake it until you make it' tips, just be the best version of yourself you can be.

"Remember back in school when the teacher told you there'd be a test? If you were like most students, you'd prepare by studying. Knowing the material makes you more confident. The same goes for networking. Want to feel more at ease? Then do your homework. Before you even set foot in a room, find out who exactly will be there. Some events make guest lists public in advance for this very reason while other times you've got to do a little digging, but in the end it's worth it. Wouldn't you want to know your number one prospect is going to be under the same roof as you so you can be prepared to speak to him or her rather than be caught off guard?

"Doing pre-event research gives you the upper hand during your interactions since the majority of people just show up and see where the evening takes them. Not you, at least not anymore! Now you come armed with information on guests, sponsors, speakers, and are ready.

"What happens when you come face-to-face with one of these people on your list? Be yourself! Don't try to sell them anything. Don't come off like a stalker and tell them all about the fascinating information you found about them online. Simply introduce yourself and start with a great lead-in question like, 'How did you find out about the event?' Or alternatively, 'What brings you here?' Then simply listen to their answer. Answers can provide countless opportunities to determine where to direct the conversation next.

"Once the event is over is when your work really begins. You've most likely got a stack of business cards and instead of tossing them in a pile, it's time to follow up. This is where most people drop the ball. They either don't do it, do it too late and the person has forgotten all about them, or you immediately ask them for something (i.e. a sale, a job, an introduction, etc.) Don't! The ideal follow up takes place the same week and these days, email is best. Send someone a quick note letting them know you enjoyed meeting them. You can ask what they thought of the event you both attended or ask them if there are any other exciting events they plan on attending. Alternatively, you can send them an article related to something you discussed or offer to make an introduction for them.

"The next time you plan to attend an event, remember the four golden rules: Read Up, Show Up (as your best self!), Listen Up, and Follow Up.

The best kind of networking is when two people connect, actively listen to one another and find mutually beneficial ways to empower one another.

"Happy Networking!"

**—Jenny Powers, founder of Running With Heels
and Podcast Host of BroadCast: Broads Building Business**

"As an entrepreneur and founder of BURU, I am a *Beyond Mom* because I am constantly working 'beyond' regular business hours. When you love your child and husband as I do, while still having a passion for your career, then you must go beyond the norm and work while others sleep. It's often exhausting, sometimes frustrating, but mostly rewarding. The flexibility to be there when my child and mate need me is priceless. If that means burning a little midnight oil, then so be it."

—Morgan Hutchinson,
mother and founder of ShopBURU

CHAPTER 8

Branding

BEYOND MOM, TO ME, IS A story about branding.

When I was a yoga instructor, people used to come to my classes because they loved the stories I told. They loved how I wove practical lessons and easy takeaways into an ancient philosophy like yoga. They liked how I never put myself above anyone else, instead staying right on level with my students, allowing us all to learn and evolve together. Once I became a mom, my pregnant yoga students and the moms who took my class felt like they got a break from the fast-paced thoughts in their head and could catch up with someone who made them feel more peaceful.

As *Beyond Mom* started to evolve, I realized the experience my yoga students had in my class was the same experience I wanted my readers to have on my website and at my events. I wanted them to feel focused, grounded, peaceful, and in touch with a like-minded community. This, in essence, is the *Beyond Mom* brand.

I hope this personal example gives you a better understanding for what a brand really is. It's not a website, it's not a business card, it's not your social media feed. Quite simply, it's the way everything you produce makes people *feel*.

Nike, through its products, makes everyone *feel* like a runner, a champion. Athleta, through its fitness clothing, makes women feel not only prepared to develop their strength, but part of a community of women, like they belong to something bigger than their individual selves. Think about Apple—they have a strong, consistent brand. Before Apple computers were ugly, intimidating, and confusing. The average person didn't look at what they had at their office or school and think, "Oh I wish I had one of those at home!" Steve Jobs built the brand of Apple around creating the opposite: making us *feel* competent and cool every time we came in touch with their product. The objects would be easy to use and gorgeous; as would their packaging, their customer support, and their advertising. The *feelings* dictated every touch point.

Far too many *Beyond Moms* skip this phase of discovery and wonder why they later feel unhappy with the look, feel, and even response to their business, even if it's generating revenue. Over time, the experience can begin to feel disjointed, and you begin to wonder *why*. Often it's because that imperative stage of discovering your brand was skipped. It can be tough to discover your brand after the business is already running, but by no means is it impossible.

Let me tell you a bit more about building the *Beyond Mom* brand. Those insights about how my yoga classes made my students feel? Those came from my loyal, regular students whom I felt comfortable asking. As my first pregnancy continued, I recognized that I didn't want to teach yoga on a regular schedule any longer, but I was certain I would create something over time. I wanted somehow to capture the experience of the people I had impacted and so I simply asked my regulars to write a brief description of the experience they had in my class. This is where my original brand language came from—from the soulful, emotional experiences my students recounted back to me. Besides getting a little ego boost (and that never hurt anybody), I discovered the core *feelings* my clients had when they interacted with me.

After that, I began a blog called randizinn.com. I wasn't sure what it was really about past my own experiences as a healthy, spiritually-minded, NYC new mom. I knew I wanted to write and provide a positive, inspiring space for my readers but I didn't know much else. My husband, who knows a thing or two about building brands, implored upon me to make the investment now in building my foundational brand. "You are going to build things over time," he said, "make the investment now so that everything you put out to the world feels unified, clear, and loyal to what you believe in. If it's done right, you won't have to 're-do' your brand for a very long time." I had no idea how right he was! Through some research and conversations, I landed upon a boutique design firm that specialized in more of a human-centered approach. I worked primarily with a designer who was also a mom and a health enthusiast. We had a meeting of the minds. It didn't matter that I wasn't entirely certain what my ultimate business model would be, because I knew what was important to me as a person, a teacher, and a content creator. After a few solid discussion sessions, a *brand* element portfolio was delivered. It consisted of a color palette, a font selection, a website design concept, and business cards. It outlined my brand language and a basic concept of sharing my content. It sounds so simple, but it was an in-depth process, and almost five years later, those brand elements remain the core of my website and everyone else I share with the world. An investment well made.

Let's dive into how you can discover (or re-discover) your brand with some questions (and musings) to get your brand-thinking moving:

What is the experience I want people to have every single time they interact with my business and me? Do I want them to feel confident? Relaxed? Inspired? Motivated? This is a place for adjectives. Keep goals and specific concepts out of here—include only the way you want people to *feel* when they interact with whatever it is you offer.

What aesthetic am I naturally drawn to? What colors? Does this inclination sync up with how I want people to feel when they interact with my brand? This is a time to study how you naturally express yourself visually and otherwise. Your brand should come naturally from you so you shouldn't take these natural expressions lightly.

I had the privilege of working with a woman named Jasmine Takanikos, a branding expert who travels the world and has created her own concept called BrandHuman—basically a way to approach branding from a very *human-oriented perspective*. Here are some of her top tips to consider as you start shaping your idea:

"It is vital to ground your idea with a foundation and framework. The BrandHuman methodology asks you to feel your way though the brand building process, while applying real time strategies. The below BrandHuman principles will support you as you begin your branding journey:

Evaluate The 'Why': Is your idea of value? Be clear on how it adds value to others.
Boundaries & Tribe: Being an entrepreneur requires a strong support network. Evaluate who you are spending your time with, are they helping you thrive? Is it time to find new community, or potentially edit out toxic people in your current circles?
Personal Brand/Positioning: How will you personally interact with the business you are building? Do you want to be public or more private? Make this decision now so you are intentional about the content you create.
Budget: Creating a cohesive brand requires an investment. You should be thinking about the following elements as essential brand building blocks: brand strategist, logo, website, lifestyle photography."

Ask for Feedback!

Just as I did, ask for feedback! If you've worked in a certain industry for a long time and you want to shift gears, it's still helpful to ask current, trusted clients to describe the experience of working with you. YOU are the common denominator, regardless of the business, so get some language about what you evoke from people. Let's say you've never run a business before. Ask your friends to share with you the ways in which they think you shine. I guarantee some of that language will bleed into the brand you're building. Survey Monkey is a great anonymous tool as well, a place to aggregate succinct questions and thoughtful responses. In one email you can ask for this essential feedback and get your responses via one portal.

My recommendation is to read through these responses several times and let them settle in. It's intense to read about yourself and it can bring up a lot. Once you've given yourself some space with this new information, create a document, perhaps an excel spreadsheet in which you create columns to categorize common themes, repeat language, etc. The repeat language (hopefully positive things) provides the insights that speak to how you naturally connect with people and share your insights. If things are not positive and are repeated, well, take note of that too and consider how you want to process that.

Looking at Your Consumer

Historically, anthropologists spent a considerable amount of time living in the midst of the communities they studied. This allowed them to truly understand the behaviors, thought patterns, and belief systems of people different from themselves and to assess them correctly. This concept is referred to as ethnographic research, in which researchers sometimes hold focus groups, discussions, or even go into the environments of the people they are studying or creating campaigns around. When you're building your brand, you must also find your own way of understanding your consumer. A good idea is not enough, in the end. You must also understand the type of individual who will engage with it and want to be part of it. I have spent considerable time getting to know the women of the *Beyond Mom* community and the great part is that it happens in the real time of my personal life as a mom as well as my work time creating content and events. Here are a few ways I've gotten to understand the "consumer" of *Beyond Mom* . . .

I talk to moms everywhere I go. Moms at the park, moms buying coffee, moms waiting to cross the street pushing their baby in a stroller, women in my workout classes. In virtually every conversation, I get some insight into what is on a mother's mind and what's relevant to her. It was in many of these early, casual discussions that I discovered how many women were both caring for their little babies and building businesses. Who knew? I also saw how little community there was for moms like these. You know how many times I heard the words, "I wish I knew more women like me! I don't fit into the stay-at-home mom world and I don't fit into the corporate working mom world, either. It would be so nice to share resources and ideas with other entrepreneurial moms!" Ask and ye shall receive.

In order to understand my consumer, I also made some general assumptions, executed on those assumptions, and then utilized the results to help me understand my potential followers further. Once I knew that entrepreneurial moms wanted to connect with other women like them, I started hosting events. For my first few events, I rented out space, got delicious hors d'oeuvres and wine, brought in an inspiring speaker, and boom, watched what happened. And what happened was magical. Business cards were swapped, coffee meetings were scheduled, friendships and collaborations were formed. After my first few events, I knew that in-person events, regardless of how much work they were, were integral to my brand because my consumer needed and wanted them. As time went on, I've gathered women in my living room for a discussion on brand-building or simply creating a space to ask for resources we might need. I'll utilize these moments to hire a photographer to snap great photos for my website but simultaneously,

I'm listening and collecting inspiration and insight on my consumer. Last year, I decided to start podcasting, knowing that the women I interviewed would have incredible wisdom to share. Clearly, I'm learning huge amounts from these women in ways that help me evolve my brand. My point is that studying your consumer can happen in real time as you are building something, but it's also key to devote real time to it.

Also important: pay attention to the buzz in your pocket of the world. If you're creating a t-shirt company for kids, read trade publications that cover kids' fashion but also understand the way that moms shop for their kids. Consider attending shopping events and chit-chat casually with the women attending. Pay attention to podcasts on entrepreneurship, business, and your specific specialty. There's so much to learn and you want to be in the know!

I guarantee the more information you can have about your consumer, the more heartfelt your product or offering will be. Some of the worst failures occur when we *think* we know what someone wants but we never really took the time to understand how things actually work and flow. When we use these products or services, we can feel that whoever made it or created it didn't really understand the need of the consumer.

Take your time, spend time, and gain understanding. It will greatly enhance the authenticity and clarity of your brand.

"Coming to understand the 'Your Soul Style Woman' was an organic process. There were parts about working as a Stylist in corporate America that I loved, and it provided practical and professional experience I still use today—but I had a strong desire to help women personally, in a very deep and purposeful way, as opposed to working for a big corporation where my contributions got diluted in hierarchies and bottom lines. Despite remaining in the corporate field for ten-plus years, it took working for five different fashion brands, and a short stint in the Masters of Social Work program at NYU to finally recognize that I needed to take the leap and start working towards building this business that I dreamed of: a mission that combined both style with mindfulness. There is fashion, and then there is style, and to me there is a distinction.

Don't get me wrong, I appreciate beautiful clothes, and the art behind high fashion, but style is the true essence of who we are at our core, without being defined by the masses. So when women work with me, we tap into that first and foremost. While there are many Wardrobe Stylists in NYC, the connection to my clients is deeper than helping them get dressed. Together we take a deep dive to discover how style begins from within. Life is full of transitions, and we are constantly evolving on every level. At times, we can lose our way, be bogged down by societal pressures, get lost in the noise of it all, become too busy to care, gain weight, lose weight, have a baby, break up, get married, change careers, or just need an overall assessment of how our deeper personality is being stylistically represented. I support women as we discover the roots of their authenticity. Only once we arrive here, can we work our way outwards to ensure the outer self-aligns with the inner one. I educate my clients to understand how personal style is relevant for an overall empowered sense of self. My clients are specific, and recognize our work is a therapeutic process, one that takes courage, and requires vulnerability and an openness to examine one's experience. Because I am personally committed to a daily practice of emotional and mental evolving, our relationship is typically a natural fit, a transference and countertransference of information, which in psychology terms means that my clients direct their feelings onto me, and I transfer emotions (with guidance) onto them. Women from all different professional backgrounds and experiences seek out my support, but many of them if not all, live mindfully, and are committed to emotional, physical and mental wellness.

I believe that a critical part of self-care is ensuring our truest self is the one that's showing up. None of us walk around naked, and clothing is a key tool in demonstrating who we are. I help my clients get there, providing a road map to authentic representation. Your Soul Style has always been a platform where style meets mindfulness, and my clients live that truth to the fullest."

**—Jenny Greenstein, personal stylist
and founder of Your Soul Style**

"When creating Mitera, I used myself as muse. I was a new mother—a working one in a corporate environment, an active one staying fit and competing in triathlons, a socially and environmentally conscious one having dedicated my life to help close the health equity gap around the world, and someone who wanted to remain stylish and feeling like myself through pregnancy and as a mom. I also turned to my close friends who were navigating the work force and motherhood.

"When building a brand, it is essential to understand your core target audience. This is why a designer often has a 'muse' whom he/she bases their designs for. I knew that, but the process for me was more organic . . . I am not trained as a designer nor do I have any background in branding, marketing, or fashion. So, I did not start Mitera thinking that I am going to build this 'brand,' though I did think through some important questions in building a brand. For me, necessity was the mother of invention.

"At the time that I got pregnant, I was working as a health specialist at the World Bank's Africa Region traveling frequently to Africa, particularly Liberia, to work on health projects. I felt there was a gap in the market for pregnant women who had to get dressed in suits and conservative dresses for work. There were some stylish solutions out there, but not many, and it seemed they were designed for women who do yoga during the day and hang out at a cafe afterward. As much as I wanted to fit into that lifestyle, it was not my reality.

"Through my brother's connection, I contacted a patternmaker in Japan who made my rudimentary sketches into two dresses that I could wear while working and pumping at the office. I wore them on a rotation, tested them, and collected feedback from fellow moms. But I didn't consider going into business for another three to four years.

"Over time, I began to use my close friends as guides when thinking about my core target audience. What are their values? How much money do they make? Where do they vacation? When are they having children? Where do they work? What do they eat? Where do they eat? Do they eat organic? Do they care about the environment? Are they well-read? Where do they shop? How do they consume information, what social and political issues do they care about? What are their biggest challenges? And so on.

"But I must tell you, we did not get everything right. We've made plenty of mistakes and we are still fine-tuning, refining, and clarifying our core brand messages, guiding us in everything from product designs to marketing to building our team."

—**Yoko Shimada, Founder of Mitera,**
a collection of clothing for professional women
who are pregnant and nursing

The Decision to Outsource Your Branding

When it comes to building your brand, there's a certain amount that you must do and understand; after all, you are the creator of the idea. But there is a point when you might decide to outsource aspects of your brand-building. Financially, this is an investment, but if done properly and with the right people, can be very fruitful.

As I mentioned before, I did do some original branding work with a design firm. To this day, I'm glad I did. I found people who understood my budding vision and that gave me confidence. At a later point when *Beyond Mom* had reached its next phase, I worked with the amazing Jasmine Takanikos, founder of Brand Human and JTCG design firm (and quoted above). It was working with her that allowed me to name not only my own skills, but to articulate the offerings of *Beyond Mom*. Sometimes you do need someone who is appropriately uninvolved to help you see the forest through the trees. Many people refer to their businesses as their "other baby," and this is entirely true. Just like we need other perspectives and insights as we raise our children, the building of our brand is no different. Here are a few tips from my own experience that might help you determine your brand outsourcing needs.

1. If you feel like you're having difficulty determining the direction of your idea and the ways in which you might want to express it to the world, consider what an external perspective might do for you. Be open, not isolated.
2. Do you like working with a team or with an individual? Like anything else, each version has a different experience with it.
3. Regardless of working with a company or an individual brand strategist, make sure you're in the midst of people who get you, your voice, and your aesthetic. A brand strategist should challenge you, of course, but also understand what's important to you at a core level.
4. Regardless of outsourcing, the more of your own work you do, the further along you will get in the project. In other words, your

understanding of your consumer, your clarity of the kind of life-style you want as you lead your company, the more educated you are in the industry, the more you can push this project along. No one will ever see the vision with as much passion as you do (after all, it's yours), so make sure you don't put your feet up.

5. Get clear about the financial investment and what deliverables you will receive at the end of the day. Be incredibly clear on all fronts so everyone knows what's what.

Whether you do this part solo or bring in external help, trust me, your early brand understanding will inform so many of your steps to come. Give it the time it deserves.

"I love the term '*Beyond Mom*' because as women we do go beyond the role of mother. We all have unique gifts and talents that transcend our pivotal position as mothers. It doesn't mean we stop being mothers or lose sight of that, it just means we can remain true to our authentic selves as well as remain the loving, connected mothers we want to be. I think we feel that somehow we have to sacrifice ourselves and our dreams in order to be mothers. Women need to be seen for who they are individually."

—Emery Chapman, mother, chef, and author of *The Heartfelt Cookbook*

CHAPTER 9

Let's Get Physical

THERE IS A MOMENT WHEN YOUR idea must become tangible—something you can touch, see, hear, or in some way, experience. In many respects, this is the birthing of your business baby because it means it's real (and you must deal with all the beautiful and challenging moments that come with it—see how much this is like your actual baby?).

I want to acknowledge that you may experience a sizeable amount of anxiety at this juncture. Consider what you've been through up until this point—you've been dreaming, discussing, designing, but never have you held IT in your hand (whatever it may be). Remember when you were pregnant and as you moved into your third trimester, you began to worry not only about the birth itself, but also about what would happen when the baby actually arrived? How much we dream of these moments and yet when their arrival is imminent, we don't always know how to explain it to ourselves. When it comes to the baby, there's no turning around. That baby is coming whether we are ready or not. But when it comes to our business, we can easily get in our own way and slow down our productivity. A self-fulfilling prophecy, some might say.

My friend Jayne, founder of Tech Tonic, a consultancy that helps people cleanse their personal and business technology, told me that she had real difficulty deciding when to transition from research to actually running a business. When is that moment? Is it after you've mapped out the revenue model? Is it after ten successful trials? Is it when you've created a website and enabled it? She asked me. There isn't one answer and each scenario is different, but what I heard from Jayne was anxiety. Let me give you a few suggestions on how to manage these moments of anxiety as you transition from idea to reality.

1. Give yourself the time to acknowledge all your worries, but be direct with them. I'm a big believer in giving room for your feelings and worries to breathe, but we can't let them take over. So perhaps give yourself one morning to sit with a notebook, a coffee, and your worries. Write them out, think through them, perhaps invite a trusted friend to listen to you talk it through. And when all the worries are out, consider which ones might be your own emotions or baggage, and which ones are issues that can be solved. List things out in detail—the more information you have, the more you can move ahead.

2. Recognize that worry is a normal human reaction to anything new and uncharted in your life. And you might need to move forward anyway. Reality: worry might just accompany you as you swim these uncharted territories. Take a deep breath and recognize it might just be this way.

3. What can you do to put one foot in front of the other? Often when we're ready to turn our idea into a reality, the *everything I have to do* concept can literally overwhelm us. Separate your lists into categories: today's list, week's list, month's list. Separate your goals into categories. Make things approachable, one task at a time. Usually, if we do things this way, we see that our anxiety over the big picture isn't necessary as we are able to tackle one thing at a time. Jayne ultimately launched when she recognized that she had nothing to lose. If she failed, then she would know that she had tried. And her

kids would get to see their mommy pick herself up and dust herself off—an extremely valuable lesson for all young people to see!

Stepping Forward

Now that we've discussed ways in which we might process our worries, let's move through them and get down to business. I'm admittedly not an expert in all types of businesses, but I'm grateful to be surrounded by some brilliant people who have had a great deal of success launching their ideas. I've done my best to garner some excellent wisdom and tip-top advice from the women I know who have started a business like yours and utilized tools to put themselves out into the world. And of course, I've thrown my wisdom in, too. I've learned a few things over these past few years! Take our insights, stories, and tools; utilize them to push your idea to its next phase of manifestation.

Let's turn our attention to the different categories of business and how we might first tackle them. Your business may straddle one or two of these categories at any given time and while the advice here might not give you every detail necessary for starting your enterprise, it will *definitely* give you food for thought as well as the grounded wisdom you need for your earliest and most integral first steps. My intention is to inspire you and light you up as you get started.

Products and Prototypes

You've decided to create a product to make the world a better place in some way, whether big or small. And a product can make the world a better place by making an experience more fun, or a person healthier or more stylish. It can even accomplish a mission like helping women return to the work force with more ease. I know so many women who had an idea based on their personal pain point or on something they simply think could be profitable! At this point in my personal career I have yet to develop a tangible product, but I speak with women all the time who have. Knowing the industry you're designing for is not a prerequisite, but having many conversations and doing tons of research is. Make sure you know *everything* about your category before you go into the prototyping process, that you understand the market for this product, the competition, the comparable products that already exist, and consider hiring a business consultant to run the numbers to make sure such a product is viable and profitable. Trust me, invest in some upfront research before you waste time and money on prototyping, only to discover the model doesn't float.

If you've discovered that you're ready to move forward, your first prototype is critical. Not only will it allow you to test your vision and how your product is made, it is the product you will use to show investors and potential clients exactly what your product consists of. You are providing the experience of your product for all parties to interact with. I've interviewed two of my favorite *Beyond Mom* friends who created incredible products based on what they discovered were missing products in their market space. They've shared their prototyping journey with me, so I can empower you.

Websites and Content

Websites have become less of a pamphlet and more of an experience: meaningful content, video series, telesummits, and more. Websites are not what they were even when *Beyond Mom* had its first go around. Websites are experiences, destinations to engage, connect, and be inspired. So what must you consider when creating a website-based company? Here are a few things I suggest you ponder:

1. What is the goal of your website? To connect people? To offer content? To engage and sell products? You must know your site's purpose before anything is designed or activated.
2. How is your brand being expressed each day via your website? All that branding work you executed now has a chance to shine, here and now. Make sure your brand is consistently expressed.

Developing our First Prototype by Heather Macdowell, Tickle Water founder, a carbonated water beverage for kids:

"In the development of Tickle Water, one thing was certain, and it was my first priority: I had to have a stand-out package. In a saturated beverage market, it was imperative that Tickle Water would command the shelf. Our product had to translate to premium, healthy, planet-friendly, clean, transparent, and 'sophistocool,' as I like to say, all in one quick visual. Tickle Water needed to be kid- and adult-friendly, but not juvenile.

"There were challenges trying to find a package that was clear, smaller in size for kids, not made of glass, and that held carbonation. I know we succeeded with our clear pet can. It feels like drinking a soda because of the pull-tab lid, but it's clear so you can see what you are drinking, and of course what's inside has the health benefits of being just clean, sparkling water.

"When building a prototype, there are always challenges. We were using a new market package so in many ways Tickle Water was the 'guinea pig.' We had labeling challenges and production set backs of course, but I just kept saying . . . 'they put a man on the moon seventy years ago, we can figure this one out!'

"I love our packaging, and that came from the process of creating our first prototype!"

3. Hire a graphic designer! There are many ways to bring in talent and not spend a huge amount of money nowadays if you're seeking a skilled individual like a graphic designer. I'm not saying you can't build your own site, but what I will say is that it can only go so far. I've learned that good graphic designers have a talent for expressing your concepts in way that is clear and elegant, and in a fashion in which others will take your work more seriously.

A story of building your first prototype, by Shelley Suh, founder of Loyal Hana, an apparel company for stylish moms through maternity, nursing, and beyond:

"When I had my daughter Cybelle in 2009, I went through the transition of redefining my life as a mother and a working woman. I went back to work four months' postpartum and in time for fashion week. I took on the role of setting up a new showroom, hiring a sales team, growing two accessory labels, and managing two license businesses. On the outside, I was a passionate career woman, strong and determined. On the inside, I struggled.

"In between my meetings I pumped twice a day in a back closet. The disparity of being a fashion V.P. and pumping in an improper facility and uncomfortable clothing left me thinking, I have to change this. At that moment, I did not realize it, but I discovered a missing market in pregnancy and postpartum-friendly clothing for women returning to their lives.

"With the pregnancy of my son Mason in 2012, I had the opportunity to work and fine tune the idea of functional clothing. My goal was to create pieces that would transition women from pregnancy to postpartum, with each item functionally providing fast and discreet access for breastfeeding or pumping.

"I had worked with many manufacturers in the past, but to realistically find someone to help develop the collection overseas, I had to create a prototype. I rummaged through stores, walked through Manhattan and Brooklyn to get inspired by street style. Finally, I sat down with a pattern maker in Chelsea, and we discussed the specs (measurements) of the prototype. I had to make decisions on how I wanted the shirt to look and, more importantly, how it would function. I contemplated different options on how to gain access to the breast and finally discovered that, for me, the zipper was most functional.

"When designing, I choose to reflect my personal style, but I also had to look at things from every level. I had to answer a lot of questions: how long should the zipper run? Should it pull up or pull down? What fabric should I use? How long should the shirt fall? Should I do long sleeve? Three-quarters sleeves? After I had discovered the answer to all these questions, in one month's time, I received my first prototype. My first instinct was, of course, to try the blouse on and at that moment I knew I was onto something great!

"A product with purpose and a clear mission helps inspire the growth.

I focused on solving an unmet need, and after two-and-a-half years, I have built a universe around the mission of the company. Loyal Hana was launched to inspire and support women. We stand behind all women as they begin their journey into motherhood and want nothing more than to provide support with a collection that not only transitions moms from pregnancy to postpartum, but also provides functionality in a chic way.

"For those of you who are working toward starting a business and trying to create your first prototype, here is my advice:

- The best resources are friends and family. I had many people in my corner helping me connect with other specialists in every profession. Use your contacts and ask for help.
- Ask a lot of questions. Don't be embarrassed if you don't know everything at first. This process is about learning and seeing how viable your product is.
- Do your research and study others with similar products. Keep product and pricing in mind. Especially what you want your target price to be.
- Once you are ready to start creating the prototype and you have identified potential manufacturers, ask for each company's portfolio. Make sure the manufacturers have the experience to do everything you need and check to see if their design aesthetic matches yours.
- Once you find a manufacturer to develop your product, request additional price quotes to determine the manufacturing charges to make the product. You will see what the standard costs and fees are in general. If one manufacturer is charging a lot more, get another quote to determine whether you are charged appropriately.
- Your prototype is your own process. Take your time and remember that the first prototype may not be perfect. It's the idea and purpose of the product that will keep you inspired to make it work!"

4. Streamline your message and do not fear white space! Avoid excess copy and clutter. Nowadays, people need to get your point quickly and visually to stay engaged or else it's on to the next thing. Keep your message clear and concise and your design aesthetic, regardless of your brand, clean and not distracting. Consider less obvious ways to express a concept. If you have a baby-related website, consider designing something other than a stork. How might the message of baby arrival be expressed in a way that is more provoking and less predictable? Your graphic designer can help you work through this.

5. What is your revenue model? If you plan to provide branded content, you must design for this type of content and perhaps for the use of high-res, professional images. If you plan to do giveaways, you must have the proper software to execute. If storytelling visually is your thing, be sure your site is designed to hold large media files. Your website must support the business model in every single way it's designed. Make sure those that are behind the scenes of your website, like your designer and your programmer, understand your business model and strategy and posses the proper experience to execute. It will help them help you!

6. Finally, consider how you will drive traffic to your website. Once again, with so many sites out there you have to get clear as to how you will direct eyes to your creation! Social media is an excellent tool to post your content and thus, direct traffic via clicks. Many websites utilize Facebook advertising to increase their views. Instagram and Pinterest (especially if you have very visual content) are excellent ways to steer traffic to your site. Twitter works well for quick, insightful ideas and for the sharing of your site's content. If your website provides a service, where can you promote that service? Where might you advertise elsewhere? What events can you be involved in or sponsor? Think out of the box. In a very saturated space, you must discover your personal message and space to command.

Service-Based Businesses

For all you moms out there who are social workers, coaches, healers, photographers, editors, consultants, and more, my questions for you are these: how do you express your unique offering? How do you differentiate from others that may offer what you do? The overwhelming and empowering truth is that there is no wrong way to share yourself and what you do with the world, there is only the way that works for you. And you must figure out how to do it in a way that validates your time and efforts. A few questions to help get you started:

1. What expression best shares your talents with those that may want to hire you? Writing? Speaking? Advertising? Word of Mouth? An example: if you are a social worker, do you begin to simply see a few clients and allow their personal recommendations feed your clientele over time? Or do you love to write about your process and share your writing with media outlets, steering more potential clients toward you? If you are a photographer, do you offer your photography for free to some growing bloggers so that your work gets out there? Or do you advertise in a wedding guide so you can start to make money shooting engagement photos? Clearly you must decide your ultimate goal and figure out how you can best share it, thus gaining clients and followers.

2. How can you put yourselves in the midst of your community? If you are a massage therapist, consider renting a space for your appointments in a wellness center where you can refer clients to one another. Attend talks and events on subjects that are of value to you. If you are an acupuncturist, volunteer your time for a pregnancy event to connect with mama-to-be clients.

3. Stay up on your expertise! There's always more info to learn, so don't get lazy. Attend trainings, read journals, and know the leaders in your field. The more relevant you are, the more clients you will be able to land.

There are many ways to share your unique perspective, so be sure to keep your mind open. So many of the women I know who have grown their unique service-based businesses have started YouTube channels, podcasts, published books, and traveled the globe speaking. Others have lived in the woods, written articles, and seen clients one at a time. There's no one way, just *your* way. Don't get overwhelmed by possibility, just meditate on what feels most natural to you. When I asked my friend Bex Borucki, founder of Bex Life and mother of five, about her experience creating her healthy living platform through her YouTube channel, her writing, and more, she shared this:

"If I had spent any amount of time watching how other people were doing it, I would have fallen into a pit of despair because everything that I was doing was so messy and so disjointed and so raw, but I think that's where my appeal lies for my followers. It really is just me doing what I do, how I know how to do it. As the years progressed and I did see this turning into a business, I did study more, I did look at other people. I gathered some tips and tricks because I wanted it to be the best platform that it could be, but I waited. I did a lot of making content and very little looking at my analytics, and I think that's a good tip for everybody starting out. This concept leads into every single part of our lives. I mean, if we are looking at our numbers on our blog, or we are looking at the numbers on the scale, or we are looking at the numbers on our paycheck, that's where our focus stays. Comparison and competition is really the undoing of all of our success, so we have to focus on what brings us joy, what makes us feel good, what we love to do. Those types of returns are most important."

What I love most about Bex's message is that she really shares her process and consequential output from a place of her own truth, what matters most to her on a personal level. Once her business began to operate with more fluidity, she started to study what tends to work in the marketplace, what might have the most return on investment. There is a balance to be struck when starting up your service-based business and that balance has everything to do with navigating from your personal compass and studying the work of others you watch and learn from. To what extent do you operate from one perspective or the other?

Regardless the vehicle of expression, keep a keen eye on your *why.* Why do you do what you do? What is the purpose of your offering? As you grow and express yourself, it's easy to get caught up in the hot new social media or new way to gain followers, but never lose track of what you seek to provide and the purpose of that offering—it's the most important truth there is!

How do you get clear on your offerings and put it out to the world?

A Non-Profit Business

I must point out that I'm titling this section as "A Non-Profit Business" for a reason! As incredible as the purpose-filled drive can be for those who start these companies that give back, they must have just as much infrastructure, strategy, and support as any other for-profit business. Many women feel called to help through something they or a family member have experienced. They genuinely want to make a difference. *Yes*, run with that, I say! But let's take another approach on non-profits. Instead of Googling how to form a 501c3, let me share with you the advice from two accomplished women I know who have been through the process of experiencing personal impact, feeling the calling, creating the community, and now, existing in the midst of a fully functioning charity. What do they have to say? What should you consider from the beginning?

I had the privilege of interviewing Sam Watson on my podcast. She is a survivor of cancer at a young age and came to discover how young adults who are struck with the disease are often set back financially, often for many years to come. She created The Samfund, an organization that provides financial support for young adult cancer survivors.

Here's what Sam had to say:

"I'll give you the advice I wish I had been given thirteen years ago:

1. Really know what you're getting into and be ready to put in the amount of time and effort! I was twenty-five, I saw a need—nobody else was helping young adults financially after treatment, and I knew from the people in my world that this was a very real need, and so I figured, 'All right, I'll do it.' I did not imagine the amount of work it was going to be, the amount of thought it was going to be, and I didn't realize either that my personal experience would only take me so far. I think many founders have such good intentions and so much passion and it's so personal, and they bank on that. That's certainly what's going to get people interested; your passion definitely comes through when you're talking about a cause that's important to you. My passion for helping young adult cancer survivors, however, didn't teach me about accounting, marketing, public relations, program development, program evaluation, and all those things are so critically important to running a successful organization. Three years into The Samfund, I went back for my MBA in nonprofit management because I needed a skillset to actually make sure The Samfund was going to be around long after people got bored with my story.

2. Do your research and make sure someone else isn't already doing your idea! There are a lot of nonprofits in this country, and chances are there's probably a program similar to what you want to do or an organization that already does it that would love your help. There's no need to reinvent the wheel. There's no need to compete with anybody else, because in the end you're competing for donors. In the end, the ones who suffer are the ones you're trying to help because now they have fewer resources available to them. The strength of each organization gets diluted."

I also spoke with Allison Stone, co-founder of the New York City-based nonprofit NYC Mamas Give Back. When her co-founder, Shana Rubin was pregnant, she passed a pregnant homeless woman on the street and was struck by how unfathomable that reality was to her. She wanted to help. The start was very grass roots: collecting baby stuff from friends and bringing them to homeless shelters. The desire to help grew and before they knew it, there were more moms involved, more stuff to donate, and there was a need for infrastructure that couldn't be denied.

Allison told me more and gave me her top tips she's learned along the way:

"For any topic that you might be passionate about but you're just not sure where to start, I suggest getting involved in an existing organization to find out more about the non-profit experience that way. Check to see if there is an unmet need. Don't repeat something that already exists!

"NYC Mamas Give Back tips for building a non-profit:

1. Build a team in which everyone cares, but everyone has varied capabilities.
2. Develop a mission with both long and short-term goals as well as a clear concept of what makes you unique.
3. Don't be afraid to ask for what you need! Ask for free stuff and reach out to your entire network. In our case, it's for helping families in need so it makes it easier to call companies and say, 'Hey, this is what we're doing. We think it's a great cause, will you help us out?'
4. Get legal help, (maybe pro-bono) with the 501c3 paperwork!"

Embracing and Growing my Service-Based Business by Hope McGrath, transformational coach and stylist

"When I decided to embark on a career transition from the fashion and art world to becoming a transformational coach, I felt a deep learning curve. Being a publicist and producer for years didn't mean I understood the art of online marketing! How would I introduce myself to the world? How could I find new prospective clients? When you are just launching your business, focus on your strengths first, then on garnering the support from mentors and coaches to advance your efforts. This was my process; otherwise I could easily be sitting alone in my home office, wondering what to do next.

Eight tricks of the trade to launch a service-based business:

1. **Get clear on your ideal client avatar.** Ask yourself key questions about your ideal customer. Age? Income? Gender? Values? Beliefs? Lifestyle? Hobbies? Your ideal client may change over time and that's okay, but you must have a clear sense of the person who will want to pay for your services. There is a big difference between fans and customers.

2. **Master your elevator pitch.** This is like a catchy personal branding overview of who you are and what you do, no longer than sixty seconds. Imagine you only have a short elevator ride to grab the attention of your dream client standing right before you. Some questions to get your juices flowing: What value do you provide? How? What's unique about your offerings? Who is your target market? Play around and make it memorable.

3. **Practice sales conversation for strong sales conversions.** The more you speak to prospective clients, the more opportunities you get for a sale. As a coach, I've discovered that the more complimentary strategy sessions I offer, the higher my percentage of increased income from private clients. Trust your intuition, present your fee with a smile, offer discounts if clients pay upfront, and believe in your self-worth.

4. **Get out there.** Engage through public speaking, partner with colleagues on their events, and attend key events as often as you can. Be bold

and speak to the person you may be intimidated by. It's the only way. If you are nervous about public speaking, push through the fear and JUST DO IT. Say NO to envy. Comparison kills joy. Embrace all those entrepreneurs rocking it in their biz (you want to be around them). Just keep doing you with steadfast focus. You will achieve your dreams.

5. **Create a killer online presence.** It's important to have a nicely designed website with simple navigation, gorgeous photos, and clear and concise copy. If you don't have an eye for fashion and photography, please get a stylist (or a stylish friend) to help clarify your look, and get a great photographer if you don't have an 'Instagram Husband.' So many women sleep on this creative process. Don't!

6. **Communicate with your audience.** Writing. Podcasts. Social media. What is your talent? When it comes to choosing the best way to communicate with your newfound tribe, start off doing what you do best. I chose to write blog posts because keeping up with social media was not my thing. Pick at least two platforms to focus on, and study up on social media strategies.

7. **Develop a Referral Program with your colleagues and clients.** Offering a monetary or service-based incentive for people to refer business to you can be very effective. I have tried various forms of referral rewards, from luxury gifts to commissions to complimentary premium coaching programs for clients who refer a friend. My clients love this incentive because they enjoy extra time working with me. One tip: be crystal clear about your referral arrangements so both parties know what to expect from one another.

8. **Don't go about this alone.** Seek out a reputable business coach or an expert mentor. We all need support and advice along the journey toward a profitable business. Ask people you trust to recommend coaches or mentors. Find out who the people you admire work with. Keep your eyes and ears open for the right match. It takes a village.

"When in doubt, trust yourself. Keep your eye on the prize and don't give up. The road is bumpy but taking risks is never easy."

What did I get from these conversations? That passion isn't enough. It's absolutely an imperative foundation to create a successful not-for-profit organization but it must be backed up by research, connections, and an ability to ask for help where you need it. There's no need to reinvent the wheel, I also learned. We'd love to save the world, but don't let your ego get in the way! If something already exists, get involved and give it everything you've got. Only start something new if the need hasn't yet been acknowledged where it can serve those who are in need.

Funding

Books are written about funding businesses and, if you spend some time on Amazon, you will find them. There are also endless articles written by experts online—read them. For now, let me just assure you that there are many ways to get initial funding, so don't succumb to the idea that because you have no starting capital, your idea should go out with the compost. Women start businesses every single day under the least likely of conditions, so keep the faith and do your research. Here are a few options to consider as you continue to manifest your vision.

Crowdfunding

Check out sites like GoFundMe, Kickstarter, and Indiegogo. These platforms allow you to create a compelling story for your idea or product, promote that story, and raise money via contributions to your project on the online fundraising platform. Crowdfunding raised approximately $34 billion in 2015. Crowdfunding is very interactive, easy to utilize, and a wonderful way to raise initial seed funding and beyond. Each platform works a little differently so read up and choose what works best for you. Also know that utilizing these platforms requires processing fees. I've contributed to numerous campaigns led by friends and connections of mine, everything from baby wearing jackets, edgy and unexpected embroidered products, to yoga studios and community spaces in distant cities. I've loved helping friends get their ideas off the ground with a small contribution, and I really love how easy it is to do it. These campaigns also work seamlessly with your social media feeds so you can easily promote what you're working toward and how to contribute.

Friends and Family

Sometimes people prefer a more private route and instead solicit immediate friends and family for their early fundraising. I've been surprised to learn that many of my favorite fitness studios and products were funded through friends and family fundraising. After all, if your friends and family don't believe in you, who will? Loved ones can invest in you through gifting you money, loaning you money, or through providing cash in exchange for equity. Understand that if you make someone an equity partner, they are basically becoming a business partner so be very clear on the terms and understanding between the two of you. Many suggest that loans are the easiest way to receive cash and fairly pay back when your business is profitable. Make sure you present your business plan and any financial arrangements with professionalism and clarity.

The risk with friends and family fundraising? Relationships. Money can bring out complicated feelings especially between loved ones, so understand with open eyes what you're getting yourself into. And you definitely can't communicate enough. If you do raise this way, keep your investors in the loop and in the know. And of course, let them know how much their support means to you by getting busy and making them proud!

Angel Investors and Venture Capital

An angel investor is an affluent individual interested in seeding a business with early-stage funding, usually in exchange for convertible debt or ownership equity. Sometimes angel investors create communities in which together they can invest in companies and also provide advice to their portfolio companies. Finding angel investors requires research and lots of conversation. Many angels invest in certain sectors so find out where and possibly with whom related companies have found their funding. Venture capital is a form of private equity that is provided by a fund or funds to early-stage and emerging companies that are deemed to have high potential or high growth rate. Typical venture capitalists provide funding after an initial seed-funding round. Venture capitalists are interested in a profitable *exit* to generate a return, such as selling a company or taking a company public. This form of funding would likely evolve as you build and recognize real momentum. Many firms in the media and tech space are funded by venture capitalists but so are concepts in the fitness, wellness, and restaurant space. Do your research and see if your growing company might one day be a candidate for venture capital funding. Don't ignore the fact that women-owned businesses don't get funded at the same rate as male-driven ones, so don't be afraid to push against the glass ceiling of the venture capital world and be the change you want to see. Women and money can (and should) work together in a healthy and growing relationship!

Self-Funding

Many women with an idea financially support it for a certain period of time. There is no right or wrong amount of money or time, but it's important that you understand how much you're willing to fund and for how long. Analyze your budget, discuss with your partner, and get clear on your values. Are you comfortable with supporting this endeavor for a year or more? Or do you need a plan to start generating some income within six months? Be realistic with your expectations as most businesses take considerable time to begin turning a profit. Consider all aspects of your business plan and if you are capable and willing to fund, embrace that blessing with information, planning, and of course, gratitude.

Your Tool Kit

There are a few items any business should consider having, whether product, content/site, service, or non-profit. Not all are imperative, depending on your goals, but all should be considered when getting ready to launch. Here's a short guide of what to consider when stocking your business tool kit and making sure those tools are sharp enough.

Business Cards

We live in a virtual world, it's true. But nothing can take the place of a beautiful business card. It's important to have that tangible item to pass to someone when either beginning a conversation, "Hi, I'm Randi, I'm the founder of *Beyond Mom* (hand card over), I'd like to tell you a bit about the important work that I do and invite you to check out my website." OR, after an amazing heartfelt discussion about mothers in the workplace at a cocktail party, hand over the card and say, "I'd love to stay in touch, here's all my info." A business card is the closer, the connector, and still to this day, says *I'm serious.* Design a business card with substance. Keep it aligned with your brand (colors, font, spacing). As always, decide to what extent you want to invest in a designed card. For me, I network a lot, so having a beautiful business card feels important. The person who designed my website also designed my card and utilized images on the card that evoke the storytelling I do on my website—the design speaks a thousand words. I also want my card to direct people to my social media feeds, so I made sure my social media handle and icons were front and foremost. Lastly, invest in good paper stock! It might seem like a small detail, but it's intriguing to watch how people take my card in their hand and say, "Wow, nice cards!" I can tell that they take me seriously when they see a beautifully designed and sturdy card. Remember, the time we take to represent ourselves speaks volumes.

A favorite online resource for ordering and designing beautiful business cards: www.Moo.com

Events

When we think about events, we tend to go big in our mind. Events can be full-blown event models (like my friend Amanda Hoffman's former company Urban Girl Squad) and partial event models (like *Beyond Mom*'s model) but they can also be small yet poignant ways to introduce you and your brand to your community. Even if your product is an online destination, consider how an event might introduce what you do or bring a good feeling to a product you'd like to share. Perhaps like I have done, utilize events as photo opportunities plus consumer research. My friends at Well Rounded NY, though they are primarily an online destination, utilize events to introduce their readers to companies and products that pay for sponsorships. Either way you utilize them, events are excellent ways to bring your brand from idea to reality. Here are a few tips to make even the simplest of events special (and speak for your brand):

❶ Don't break the bank, but always provide lovely drinks and nibbles. A bottle of wine, sparkling water, lemon slices, cheese, almonds, and crackers. Maybe some fruit. This always goes a long way. If you have glassware and pretty plates, wonderful. If you choose to go disposable, there are so many beautiful products nowadays that can still feel classy. Check out one of my favorites, www.susty.com. Whole Foods puts together very nice fruit and cheese platters, but consider placing the contents on a ceramic platter with fresh flowers—it brings your offering to another level.

The point is that you want to welcome people wholeheartedly to anything that you host. You are constantly representing your brand. It's the simple efforts that go a long way, trust me.

It's worth noting that many companies would be thrilled to sponsor your events by sending drinks, snacks, products as gifts, and more. At the very beginning you may need to front some costs, but as your gatherings have a bit more momentum and you have some photos to prove it, don't forget to save costs by having companies provide many of these event assets. It makes everything more enjoyable and will save you the extra expense. And you develop relationships with all sorts of companies that will get to know you and be happy to support your endeavors.

2 If you host your event in your home, clean up and put the kids toys away. Create an adult environment. Unless of course, it's a kids event. Then decorate and create the fun appropriately. If you host outside your home, seek a location that fits your budget or perhaps negotiate a free space if you consider promoting the offerings of your host location. Be creative. You never know who might want twenty-five new faces to walk through their door! Don't forget to seek our sponsors for your décor and craft needs!

3 Take pictures! No matter what. Your events, no matter how big or small, represent the way you connect with people. And without people, we have no businesses. If the event is small and simple, generally your iPhone will do. If you plan to utilize these photos on a website and even quite a bit on social media, consider a photographer or at the very least, a friend who owns a professional camera and is pretty good at using it. High-resolution photos look a million times better. Whenever I've hosted an event and hired a professional photographer, I've always been so glad. Over time, I've built a portfolio of images that represent the way I have connected my brand with people. I've used these images over and over both for content and social media—they're a good investment. These photos will also be the means by which you secure those sponsors I mentioned, the proof that you are legit and that people are gathering around whatever it is you're creating!

Social Media

To me, social media is the storytelling tool of our brand and does make our product or service come alive. I've watched how many of the mom entrepreneurs in my life have utilized social media to grow (and succeeded) while others struggle to understand how to make it work for them. There's no doubt that it's one of the greatest tools we have to reach a wider audience but it does require some kind of strategy, even if it's a simple one. Here are a few important questions and suggestions as you embrace your brand's social media presence.

1. What is your brand and product, and which social media outlet(s) will best represent your brand? Between Facebook, Twitter, Pinterest, Snapchat, and Instagram, we could spend all day on social media. But then we might not have a business. Or any real friends. It's important to consider your product and which social media outlet best expresses it. If you are a chef or a health coach, you might want to focus your attention toward Instagram and Pinterest because they are visual tools. If you have content or a mission, focus toward Twitter as you can easily share articles, quotes, and inspiring information. Get clear on where you can best utilize your time and express the best version of your brand story.

2. If you're going visual, use great images. You can probably already tell that I'm a fan of good, quality photography. You don't need to invest in a professional camera or photographer if it's not in your budget or high on your priority list, but you do need to post only nice pictures. It amazes me how frequently I see people post dark, blurry, and unattractive photos on their company Instagram page. Folks with larger social media following would never post a poor-quality photo. Most people or companies with a larger following have a distinct aesthetic in mind, dictating the images they'd consider posting or not. Their look is unified, clear, and usually bright. And this is attractive, and why people often click the "follow" button. Download a free editing app and use it to brighten and fix any image you post. It's worth the few extra minutes. My favorite editing app is called Snapseed. Find it in the app store for free.

❸ I'm speaking to the mom part of you now. We know our kids are cute. We know that cute kids sell. But resist the urge to post pictures of your kids all over your brand social media, unless applicable to your business message. I like to view our kids as complements to our lives (and obviously, our personal Facebook page is an excellent place to plaster as many pictures of our little ones as we like), and our kids may even be part of our brand (perhaps we are designing a kid's t-shirt line or a snack product for picky eaters). But I believe it's important to separate your product, its story, and how you share it, from a million pictures of your kids. I sometimes wonder, as well, what our kids will say to us down the road when they see how much we shared of them to the public. I'd never want my kid to feel overly exposed in a way they can't fully explain. We live in a public world via social media but it can and should have limits. As mompreneurs, we need to know those limits and fold them into how we represent our brand. At *Beyond Mom*, I include my children minimally. They make a photo if they are part of expressing the way that I juggle my life or a *Beyond Mom*-esque anecdote, but there's not that many straight up cute photos for cuteness sake. Those are saved for my personal Facebook friends. Could I gain more followers with thousands of cute kiddie pics? Probably. But I want my followers to be engaged for the right reasons, and for me, that's women who want to live a balanced, inspired life while building their dreams.

Arielle Haspel is a certified health coach and healthy chef. She owns a company called Be Well with Arielle, where she shares healthy recipes and lifestyle tips. She also has a few online cooking shows. Follow her on Instagram at (@bewellwitharielle).

Here is what has helped Arielle build her following:

- **Be ME.**
  "Whether it's a photo or quote or experience I'm sharing, it must feel really good to me when I press 'share.' Being authentic and speaking in my voice feels the best to me. Remember—people will like you more for being yourself.

- **Be Consistent.**
  "I always intend to keep my message consistent. My social media account is all about healthy lifestyle. Anything personal or business-related that I post, is always, in some way, healthy lifestyle/positive thinking/food-related. Just like you (I'm sure), I follow certain people for certain reasons. For example, I just moved into a new apartment so I'm following interior designers with content that I admire. When they veer off and start posting other content that is (way too) personal, like photos of their kids making snowmen, I find it annoying. If you're trying to build a business, stay focused on your message and consistent with your messaging. Give people what they expect from you and you'll have happy followers.

- **Be of Value.**

  "In every post, I like to be of service in some way. Inspiring people to cook at home, supporting people on their health journeys, finding positivity in their lives. When I'm of value to others, it feels really good. Ask yourself: how can I be of service to others?

- **Be Strategic and Scheduled.**

  "Post relevant content to the time of day that you're sharing something. I'm more apt to post a breakfast recipe at 7:00 a.m., than a burger recipe. When I wake up in the morning and see photos of burgers, it's just not appetizing! Before you post, imagine your followers at their computers and behind their phones. What do they want to see from you?"

"As any woman who is a wife, a mom, and a company founder, I place great care and effort in balancing these three aspects of my life. I strive to pay attention to details and make things and moments meaningful, beautiful, and memorable. I do this in my relationships as well as the products I design at PaperGirl Collection."

—Ana Bianchi, mother, founder of PaperGirl Collection

CHAPTER 10

Staffing Up

WHEN I FIRST STARTED BLOGGING AND was also still managing my late father's business matters, my husband suggested I hire someone to help me "manage my stuff." "What do you mean?" I asked, incredulously. What in the world do I need someone to help me with my stuff for? At the time, I simply couldn't imagine letting someone into my personal matters or even into the small blogosphere I was building. In retrospect, I had no idea how helpful it can be to have someone touch the details of my life, to help me organize things or think through solutions to things that just felt messy. I felt like everything needed to be on my terms and therefore in my hands, for them to be right.

"Trust me," my husband said, "once you get some help, you'll understand how useful it is. You won't turn back." I had no idea how right he was. I don't want to give the impression that having people work for me and my *Beyond Mom* business has always been easy; if anything, it's been the opposite.

Like any relationship, it has exposed my vulnerabilities, forced me to face my weaknesses, and forced me to own my voice.

Like dating, it takes time to find the right fit, no matter what the role. It requires you to be organized about what you need and to find that balance between being yourself and having boundaries—something super hard for me to do. Let me tell you more about my journey of inviting people into my work world.

Not long after my husband encouraged me to find some help, I realized that my database was a mess. *What a good place to start*, I realized. A young woman I crossed paths with and was an eager production assistant on a documentary film (let's call her Anna) was happy to give me some hours each week. We met once a week for a few weeks and she basically helped me feel more organized and aligned with the moving pieces of my life. She was prompt and responsive, and helped create the foundation I could jump from. Working with her taught me some good lessons, ones I carry through to this day:

❶ Don't hold so tight to your matters that they begin to burden you. Find someone who you believe is trustworthy and get some help getting things in order. Something might seem so complicated to you, but in the end, it's really not.

❷ Inviting help into your life ultimately will make you feel more clear, but most importantly, it allows you to keep your eye on the ball (and the ball is the work that only YOU can do). Consider what tasks you can pass on to someone else and what time that would free up for you. I really believe that once I got organized, my mind cleared out for more inspiration to rush in.

❸ Having someone work for you is excellent management practice and forces you to step it up. When you are only accountable to yourself, things can get a little lazy. When someone looks to you to be productive, suddenly you are more productive yourself. Also, let's face it, when you have to fork over some moolah, even if it's a relatively small amount of money, it forces you to pay closer attention to everything you're doing.

Anna got married and moved onto bigger and better things and at that time, I was ready to launch a newer version of my website. I had also recently discovered that I was pregnant. My husband had a friend who was looking for more creative work; she also had a blog of her own and seemed to know a thing or two about social media. We met, we clicked, and we agreed to work together. For the purposes of this story, let's call her Mara. Without a doubt, Mara helped me create the next version of my site and encouraged me to own my voice as an NYC Mom who cared about certain things and wanted to write about them. She had an excellent visual aesthetic and taught me the basics of having a voice on social media. For all of that, I'm grateful.

The unfortunate part of the story is that I hadn't yet developed my chops as a manager. I wasn't sure exactly how to create the right boundaries with someone who worked for me and ended up feeling like I was in a *friend zone* more times than the *work zone*. I always felt like I was subtly being taken advantage of, not because Mara was a bad person, but because I wasn't mature enough to fully ask for what I needed and insist upon its completion. I'd use the word "sloppy" to describe that period of time. It's not that nothing was happening, it's just that it all could've been so much better.

As in any relationship, frustration grew and I felt our relationship shifting. I knew it was time for a change but I just wasn't sure what the next phase would look like. Luckily, I'd begun working with my branding strategist at around this time, and she assured me I would find someone else who could support this next phase. As luck would have it, Mara had opportunities that took her out of town, so even though I did have to let her go, she was sort of *going* anyway. This working relationship took me all the way to the point that I realized *Beyond Mom* was really what it was, so Mara was really part of me *figuring it out*.

That period of my working life and this relationship taught me some huge lessons:

❶ Boundaries are crucial. When it's just you and another person dreaming up ideas together, it's really easy to get super personal.

Personal is okay, but only to a point. Women love to connect but it's true that when there is money exchanged, when work is on the line, it's not appropriate for everything to be exposed.

2 Listen to your gut. I felt off about my working relationship with Mara for way longer than it took me to vocalize it. There's plenty of moments I should've opened up my mouth, expressed my frustration, and asked more questions. But it's through this frustration that I've learned these hard lessons. As women, we too often smoosh our feelings down and assume they aren't worth listening to. On the contrary, as women and mothers, our intuition is razor sharp, and we should always slow down and pay extra close attention to what it's saying.

3 Don't let your weaknesses control a situation. If I'm being honest, I felt like the fact that I was a new-ish business person was taken advantage of by Mara. But I allowed this situation to occur. Why? Because I didn't have confidence in myself. Confidence, I've realized, doesn't mean that you know it all or that you have to. Confidence comes from deep inside of you, from your core, and it says "I am a strong, capable person. That which I don't know yet, I will learn. But I am logical and worthy of leading what I care about." This is the kind of confidence that doesn't allow anyone to push you around.

When I moved on from Mara, I felt clear about the kind of individual I wanted to work with. I wanted to feel like I could be myself (honest, silly, strong-willed, and sometimes indecisive) but also be clear that work was our primary priority. I wanted to be around someone that respected me for the hard worker I am, that showed up excited and positive and had a good heart (as well as a smart mind!). Similar to how I felt when I met my husband, I had kissed enough frogs to know what I no longer wanted and was pretty clear on the kind of guy I wanted in my life. I believe that to manifest any good relationship, we need to be pretty clear about what we don't want, and super clear about what we DO.

Now, when I met Aileen, she immediately expressed herself as all the things I was looking for. She was communicative, passionate, hard working, and willing to do anything to get *Beyond Mom* growing. I thought I was hiring a community manager, but several years later, Aileen is also my think partner. We talk about everything, and it's wonderful to have someone by my side who I enjoy working with so much. We'll talk more about what a *Beyond Mom* business is, but let's just say, we've worked in the midst of tantrums, nursing, my tears, her tears . . . we've worked through *life*. And yet, even in the vulnerability of it all, we still know we're there for work. And even when we've had to discuss money, or worries about company direction, or any of the subjects that can cause anxiety, we speak openly to one another and get through it. My work relationship with Aileen has showed me that I can be ME but also have a work relationship that operates primarily for the purpose of work. It's showed me that you can actually love a person that works for you, as long as everyone understands that work is priority. I've learned that I can be myself and still have healthy boundaries. Aileen and I continue to work together as I write this, and I hope we continue to for a very long time! It will certainly be interesting to see how the company grows and evolves and what it would feel like to have even more employees working with us, and that's a growth I know we're both up for when the day comes. A few tips I've learned by working with Aileen:

1. I can be ME and still be a leader. Yes, I can be nice, friendly, and sweet, and also be serious, direct, and clear about my needs. When you feel confident for the right reasons, relationships tend to be more in balance and if they are not, you move on. Aileen has given me a real life example of the right balance in a working relationship.

2. If everyone is honest, everyone can grow. I haven't been at the place to hire Aileen full-time, but Aileen needs to make full-time money. Our dialogue on that has been open. I constantly have my ears open and have brought lots of part-time work to Aileen through the *Beyond Mom* community, enough to keep her in the place she needs

to be financially. I've assured her that I can't wait to hire her full-time (when the business need is really there and revenue supports it), but I do my best to make solid connections for her. It's a mutual relationship based on honest communication. And that is key.

3 Speak up! Women don't always have this part together. If something bothers us, we keep quiet. If we want something done differently, we hesitate to share why. Just as we must tell our kids what we expect of them, we must do the same with our working relationships. I've learned that as clear and honest as I can get with my expectations, the better everything goes. The work output is better and our employee feels motivated because they understand what is expected of them. Don't hold back, speak up!

I've shared an awful lot about my personal experiences staffing up *Beyond Mom*. This is a story that will unfold as my company and I grow. I share all of this nitty-gritty with you because I think we all go through some version of it and can relate to it. You are not alone in your struggle. So now that we know that, let's discuss some of the things you must analyze as you consider bringing people onboard.

What Do You Need?

In order to know who to hire and how often to make them available to you, you must know what you need. Make a list of the things that must get done. Make a list of the things you hate to do and a list of the things you love the most (the parts of your work where you feel you shine). Compare these two lists. An easy concept is to consider outsourcing the tasks that burden you and don't need to be done by you. What can easily be passed over to someone else and will thus free you up to work your unique magic?

You must, of course know how much you're able to spend. What is your budget for outsourcing any of your work at this period of time? What can you afford? And that's a more complex question than just looking at a spreadsheet. Sometimes you have to invest in help for the mundane stuff to free yourself up to make the big vision decisions that will grow your business. If I'm tethered to my desk performing basic client services, I'm not out attracting new business. So while I might be losing X dollars an hour on an assistant, I am potentially making triple that in those freed-up hours.

A good rule of thumb is to look at what you are making an hour. Everything that costs less than that—outsource. Everything that is more, look at as a growth opportunity and learn to do yourself until your billables grow to the place you can take them off your plate.

Also consider the kind of work environment you want to create when bringing another individual into the picture. If you like having someone around and feel energized by another human energy, consider how often you might work together and where. If you absolutely feel drained by another person's energy when you're trying to focus, consider a virtual assistant (more to come on that option). There's no right answer on this one; there's only your answer. Let your needs guide this process.

A Few Hiring Options Once You Decide What You Need:

Virtual Assistance

A virtual assistant (typically abbreviated to VA, also called a virtual office assistant) is generally self-employed and provides professional administrative, technical, or creative (social) assistance to clients remotely, from a home office. Most virtual assistants are contract or freelance workers who do their jobs from home and focus on administrative tasks that are similar to those of an executive assistant or secretary.

This can be a wonderful option for someone who needs the organizational or the creative assistance but doesn't want the overhead of office space or full-time employee costs. It's a direct route to get the support you need as you grow your concept without the extras. It's also a great option for those who like to work solo and don't necessarily want another individual in their workspace.

A few suggested sites for finding a virtual assistant:

- www.upwork.com: good for freelance online projects!
- https://www.zirtual.com: for a monthly membership you can have your own virtual assistant to assist in all aspects of your life.
- https://www.redbutler.com
- https://www.fancyhands.com

Point? There's so many ways to clear off your desk, cross items off your to-do list, and open up your flow for your genius. Take a peek at some of these options and imagine how the right support will project you forward.

Assistant Sharing

This is where your network comes into play. Have a mompreneur friend who also needs some support? Consider sharing the same support person to have access to someone with skill but also to ease up on the budget. This allows you to have continuous support from the same person over time, in person, as opposed to a person that you might not get to know as intimately. Consider what it means to spend time with someone in person and if that's what you want, an assistant share might make sense. Like anything else, clarify with your mompreneur friend on exactly the type of individual you both need and the process in which you'd each like to engage. Ask tough questions, determine your flexibility (if one of you needs your assistant one week for an event, are you willing to sacrifice on some hours?). Or do you each agree to pay overtime if your needs require it?

Part-Time

Finding part-time support is a perfect segue to the next level of your business. It allows you to experience the effects of clearing off your desk and to-do list, of getting support with your social media if you need it, of having some help with your inbox, or of coordinating the details of an upcoming event. Understand that working with someone part-time means they will also have other work-oriented commitments and/or potentially be hunting for something full-time. Be open to the person's situation and also be clear on your expectations of the hours they are paid for.

Your network is one of the best ways to find a part-time person, as well as many of the websites in which you can post for positions. Graduate schools can also be a great place to land intelligent, driven students who want to make money while they achieve their degrees. Don't forget the moms you know who might want to give fifteen hours a week to something that also allows them to be with their kiddos—ask friends who they know!

Full-Time

A full-time employee has the most burden financially but potentially the most return. When you hire a person full-time, be sure you understand the legal requirements in your state. Understand that you must be aware of providing health insurance and other necessary benefits like social security, severance, payroll tax, and more. If you are hiring someone full-time, you should have the advice of an attorney and an accountant. You need to be sure you are well-organized and doing things properly. The way you organize your employees sets the tone for the work you produce and the way you interact with your clients. Take the process very seriously.

Personal Considerations

Recognize that when you hire any help, you are hiring a human being. Humans have health issues, family worries, and finances. They are not perfect (just as you and I are not perfect) but that does not mean you shouldn't have high expectations. Make sure your expectations are realistic, but also that this person is a valuable addition.

As moms, our personal often bleeds into the professional. If our nanny calls out sick, a meeting might need to be cancelled or moved to the living room couch. Phone calls might happen with some kiddie screeching in the background. I've had a few frustrated, emotional breakdowns with my co-worker. Make sure you're working with people you feel comfortable with and who are willing and able to be flexible. As *Beyond Moms*, flexibility is a main ingredient to our productivity. Make sure the people you bring on understand that.

Letting Go

Letting someone go is one of the most dreaded moments in business. And I must say, not one of the strongest skills for most women. It's in our nature, generally speaking, to nurture, develop, and support the needs of others. We often put our personal needs second and, therefore, even in business, hold on to people a little longer than we should. There's a million reasons why we know deep down that it's time to let someone go—budget cuts, change in business model, or a simple "this person just isn't the right fit." You can also simply outgrow an individual. What worked a year ago, might not work now. If you are entering business on any level, you will unfortunately have to inform people that you will no longer need their services and you will have to manage the icky feelings that go with it. I have had to do it more times than I like, and I know I will have to do it again. It's part of business life. So breathe into it.

Remember how I told you I inherited my father's businesses? That included a group of employees, many of whom I had known since my youth. Several of them had never worked for anyone else but my family. None wanted to lose their positions but knew that things would somehow change. Several years after his passing, one of his businesses had been sold, another had simply stopped pursuing projects, and what remained (basically land, buildings, that general aviation airport, and a small storage unit business) required only a few employees to manage. I knew that this team needed to be tight, focused, and title-less—in other words, all hands on deck. After analyzing budget and team dynamics, it was clear that several people had to go. But these were people I had known since I was a teenager, who had hung out with me at my home, who had families of their own and depended on their jobs. But, what could I do? I could no longer justify their position nor the dynamics that had evolved in the group. *Something had to change.*

One employee in particular was extremely emotional and worried about losing her job; one summer day she sent me an email to the effect of, "I sense something is wrong. Am I losing my job?" I knew it had to be addressed, and I had to work through the challenge, rather than avoid it. I met with her that day and through a rapidly-beating heart and tears that couldn't help but fall, I sat next to her and told her that indeed, things were changing. This situation wasn't overly rehearsed, and I didn't have all my ducks in a row, but I told her that she still had a job for another year. In this case, she was an employee for over twenty years, someone who had been devoted for a very long time, and that is always to be considered. I told her that she would have the freedom to interview during that time and that I was committed to paying her for that full year (this functioned as a severance). She cried but also admitted to a sense of relief, finally knowing that the vibes she felt were real and not based on a figment of her imagination. This story is not one that illustrates perfect delivery or a package tied up in a bow. This one represents an honest, messy, real life moment. Sometimes they can't be avoided.

A few tips in navigating the inevitable firing process when it does arise:

- Before you even start to think about what you're going to say, educate yourself on your state laws. Every state has different laws around employment so make sure you're familiar with what applies to you and your situation. If you're unsure and even if you are, consider an attorney who can enlighten you. The next thing you want to consider is timing. Does it make sense to give someone a long notice period? Or is today their last day? What kind of severance is fair? I like to be certain that I treat everyone fairly as it creates good karma, and you don't want to leave someone in a very bad financial situation. With that being said, you must do what you feel is right for all involved when it comes to severance and compensation.

- When it comes time for the sit down, the best path is to rely on clarity and compassion. When the time comes to sit down, no matter how frustrated you have been to get to this point, don't waffle, but don't be mean, either. This is a moment that is testing your brand, and you want to look back and feel it was handled well. Clarity with your words is primary. Don't say more than you need to. Compassion is primary as you must understand the emotional experience of the person being let go. It's not your job to own their emotions, merely recognize that they are there, they are real, and give the person room to experience them.

- If you are letting someone go, you do not need to tell them everything about *why.* I have been in positions where I share just enough information for the person to have closure, but not too much to overexpose myself or make the conversation more confusing and emotional. When we are nervous, as we might rightfully be in a situation like this, we might talk too much. Breathe deeply, take notes, rehearse what it is you need to say, talk it through with a trusted friend. Sharing only what you need to is not dishonesty, sometimes it's the best way to navigate a difficult moment for both parties.

Letting someone go is one of most trying moments for any business person. I've had some good, sobbing, belly cries after I've had to do it. Why? Because letting go is hard. Hurting someone is hard. But business is business and this is one of the challenges that accompany it. If your facts are in line and your ethics are clear, you should be able to navigate these moments with grace—no matter how much we dread them.

Most importantly: own your right to make changes, to move on, to change your mind, to disappoint someone. Own your voice. It must be used both as a mom and definitely as a *Beyond Mom.*

"I once found myself in a cab between meetings and struck up a conversation with a driver who explained that he drove the cab by day, then bartended at night to make ends meet. He called bartending his 'second shift.' It struck me that I was doing my own version of being a cabbie/bartender. I was doing Human Resource training and consulting by day; followed by my 'second shift' of admin items such as research, calendar scheduling, and bookkeeping, by night between 7:30 p.m. and midnight, when my toddler twins were asleep. Most of our consultants and vendors have always been women. When I jumped online at night, I felt like I was part of this unspoken world of women working their 'second shift.' I was struck by how many did serious work during this 'second shift': networking, brainstorming, and solving problems. While I discovered that if I ate a whole foods diet and walked two miles in the morning, I could sustain my energy level for weeks on only five to six hours of sleep per night, I realized it was not a sustainable business model. It became abundantly clear five years after we launched that I needed to surround myself with people who were able to take administrative tasks off my plate and run with them, freeing me up to focus on more strategic pieces of the company like recruiting more consultants, speaking to clients about potential projects, and delivering consulting projects myself. I realized that in order to grow I needed to find a bookkeeper and virtual assistant. Once they were both in place, it was then that I was able to scale. This allowed me to have the business run whether I was in meetings, facilitating training at a client location, or volunteering at my twins' school. My realization: every time I invested in a new team member, the business ultimately grew.

"Tips I've collected on my own hiring journey:

① When you first launch, check in with folks you think of as your 'personal board of directors,' a group of less than five family and friends that you trust to guide you, review marketing materials, and serve as a sounding board for your ideas. Keep this group close to you as you grow.

2 Consider the administrative tasks you can outsource to someone who is expert at those items, such as bookkeeping, scheduling, organizing an event, and sending out holiday cards.

3 Make sure your first hires are the right culture fit, as they need to be an extension of your personal brand. When you first start, the brand is you, and clients are often buying from you because they trust you. Therefore, these first hires need to have the ability to tell your story, represent you in written communication, and share your optimism in the company.

4 Always hire people smarter than you in what they are smart at. Then get out of their way.

5 When you are in growth mode, it feels indulgent to slow down and plan. This is, however, a critical step. I suggest having periodic meetings with yourself to be still and make sure things are not just growing, but growing in a direction that honors the original reasons you started the business."

6 Keep a delusional belief in your idea, and never, never, never give up."

Making it a *Beyond Mom* Business

I RECENTLY HAD A HEARTFELT CONVERSATION with a dear friend who is a devoted wife, a mother of two little girls, an incredible friend, and a skilled acupuncturist. She was reflecting on how challenging it is to feel like there is even one moment for her to consider herself in the equation of her life. "I so naturally put everyone else first, my own needs are something that get factored in after the fact. I always feel like I'm catching up with myself, working to quickly ground, focus, and mostly, to be present and grateful each day." I assured her, as I assure myself, that all of us, at this particular stage of motherhood and business development, struggle to make contact with our own needs. It can feel like an uphill battle and one in which you don't always feel like the best version of you is the battle leader. Fear not, my *Beyond Mom* friends. We are in this together. There are millions of us still in the thick of our motherhood experience while also seeking the rest of our life to be productive and purposeful. The part that makes the experience a *beyond* experience is that there is a desire to do things with consciousness and clarity. We want to be present, we want to be grateful, and we want our lives to amount to something more than the daily motions. We want to have something of our own. But we don't want to leave our mom selves at the door when we enter our working, creative mode. We want all parts of ourselves to be recognized and present as we create something.

This concept is possible. Really, it is. But it must be created with the practices that support the integration of the different parts of our lives. It must be supported by a foundation that is strong and steady, in our mind, our body, our spirit, and our community. We cannot do it alone, so we must attract other strong, supportive individuals that will lift us up. We must be realistic about what it will look like daily, weekly, monthly. What we are working on building is not a fantasy, but very much a realistic experience developed every single hour of every day. What anchors it are the very practices I have been weaving throughout this book, suggestions for you to consider so that you are *not* lost, weak, or worried. And most of all, these practices will ensure that you will be successful, both personally and professionally. Now that you have recognized what it means to go beyond and what is required, let's discuss how to weave these concepts and practices into the *Beyond Mom* business you're building.

Tuning In through Mindfulness

For many moms, and particularly very busy moms doing the juggle between family life and entrepreneurship, we somehow lose touch with our innermost life, the voice that gives us direction, desire, the voice of our personal clarity. *I don't know what I want anymore*, many moms tell me. What they know is they are dissatisfied and seeking more. For a *Beyond Mom*, making contact with that inner self is incredibly important because if we are going to go beyond, we have to have an inner compass, a sense of that which serves us or doesn't. Achieving the ability to both pursue a creative vision and raise our children in a way that satisfies us cannot be done without a very key concept—and that is *mindfulness*. What is mindfulness? Mindfulness is a practice in which we know how to slow ourselves down enough to listen. What we hear is the information we utilize to make sound and grounded decisions in our lives. Achieving mindfulness allows us to step out of that victim state that so many busy moms find themselves in, the sense that life is moving at a faster pace than can be kept up with, that we can't make sound decisions for our own lives. The simple achievement of mindfulness allows us to get our feet on the ground and our inner ear open to our truth. When we operate from that place, we hear what Gabby Bernstein calls our inner guidance system, or our intuition. Quickly, our priorities rise to the top and we see what they are, magnetically drawn toward them because we understand they are what we should be working toward. By the way, this is advice that every single human needs in today's day and age, in this fast-moving, plugged-in culture. But it's especially necessary for the *Beyond Mom* who constantly switches hats, cares for so many, and wants to achieve so much. Here's how I have brought mindfulness into my life:

1. I use breathing to slow down my thoughts and manage my anxiety. It's no secret that harnessing the breath is an ancient tool to achieve oneness with self. But for a busy mama, this concept of meditation or pranayama (as the breath practice is referred to in yoga) can feel like another thing to add to the to-do list. I've found that if I can assign an intention to it, it's something I can work into my daily life, something I can do even when I'm walking down the street. If I'm feeling anxious or overwhelmed, I tell myself to start taking longer, deeper breaths that move from my belly to the top of my head. It's incredible how after a few rounds of conscious breathing, the thoughts racing through my head slow down, the issues worrying me feel more approachable, and over time, I've even come up with solutions in this post-breath work space. When can you fit in a few minutes of deeper, focused breathing? Walking down the street works for me; for nursing mamas, it might be when you're nursing or rocking your baby to sleep. It might be when you're doing menial household chores that don't require too much thinking. In these moments, begin your deep breathing, being conscious of

what you want to achieve through this activity: managing anxiety, focused thinking, new ideas. Over time, I've realized that *Beyond Moms* usually possess the personality type that needs something specific to work toward, which is why this focused, goal-oriented breathing can work better than just breathing for breathing's sake. Use tools like Headspace to achieve ten minutes of mindful breathing a day. It has helped me considerably!

2. Manage your technology use (and abuse). I'm so guilty of overusing my iPhone. It feels like a portal to the world I'm creating and the way I connect to the outside world (thanks social media). It's even the way I check directions, check the weather, get up to the minute world news and inherently during those tasks, I check my email, Instagram, and Twitter feed. It never stops, does it? I honestly think we need people to call us out. Like the other night when my husband snuggled up next to me on the couch to relax and catch up, and still, I was surfing the social media world. "Put the f-ing phone down babe," he said as he pulled me toward him. YES. *Put the f-ing phone down*, everyone. I realized recently that I was spending a bit too much time taking videos of my life so I was missing out on being fully present in beautiful moments in real time (thanks, Instagram stories!) I'm a fan of social media and the many ways it can help us stay connected with people we love and expand our business reach, but our only hope *not* to miss our lives is to put the f-ing phone down! Monitoring our own behaviors and habits are a major way to stay mindful. When we are online, we are not in tune. It's true. If we seek to feel clear-minded and on top of our own needs, we have to make the space for that clarity. But how do we do it when it feels like the world asks us to connect (with our phones)? Similar to how we must manage our calendars and our commitments, we must have some rules around our technology use. Many of the *Beyond Moms* I chat with put the phone aside during the evening hours, usually between dinnertime, bath time, and bedtime. This allows them to really be with their kids and be mindful with that time. So many

complain that they never feel fully with their work or fully with their kids and, sadly, we do this to ourselves. If we decide to put the phone away for two hours of time with our kids, trust me, that time will feel potent and delicious. When we come back to our work once they are in bed, we will really be able to focus on it and might accomplish more in less time. It's a win-win, but it does take discipline. The result? Presence, and therefore mindfulness, accompanied by the feeling that we are absorbing each moment of our life in a real way.

A perfect meditation for *Beyond Moms*, from my friend Bex Borucki:

"My favorite mantra is: 'this moment is mine to make brand-new.' You can expand on it with: 'no matter where I've been, no matter what I've done, no matter who've I've been or what's happened to me, it does not define who I am.' This moment is mine to make brand-new. I try to approach every day with that. Every day is a new beginning and you are definitely informed by your past and what you've learned, but start fresh. You yelled at your kids—take a pause, that's what meditation is. It's just a pause in your day to contemplate, to breathe, to be with yourself, to say you are worthy of taking a little bit of time to pay attention to, so you take that pause and you move on."

Balance

Balance is a sense that no one part of our life is dominating another, that every part of our existence gets its equal and necessary time. When we have achieved balance, we feel a certain sense of peace, like we can breathe easier and the many parts of ourselves have room to grow and evolve (our friendships, our professional life, our physical fitness, our spiritual life.) When we were single and especially before we had children, we had so much more time to achieve the emotional experience of balance on a personal level. Though we might've complained how busy we were, we now understand that the space we had was indeed a luxury—that most parts of our lives were acknowledged, and much more often. Many busy moms (and dads, too) think back on those days of freedom and get sucked into a sense of nostalgia, of how free and happy they once felt. This causes an all-too-often sense of longing, and even frustration for some of us. It's not that we want to give our kids back, but we just wish we could experience that feeling of balance more often, and that we were making some sense of headway.

Achieving balance as a *Beyond Mom* requires something that is very crucial; it's called a mindset change.

Just as we must accept that things have changed, we must accept that the old version of balance has set sail and a new kind is the one we must seek.

That's right, it's not going to look like it once did, so let's take a deep breath and accept it once and for all. *But* . . . a new sort of a balance IS possible. Some call it integration, some call it flow, others call it a relay, different strides at different moments. We can define in it in whatever way it makes sense to us individually. The point is that we form a new relationship with our idea of balance so we can feel satisfied with our results. Indeed, all parts of ourselves can get some attention—it just might look different than it used to.

A favorite story of mine: several times a year, I co-host an incredible daylong retreat for moms called *Finding the Om in Mom*. True to its name, we spend the day both physically and mentally bringing ourselves back to a sense of calm and inner ease, giving space for all parts of ourselves to open up. During our circle discussion, one of our retreat participants who was a mom and elementary school teacher, admitted that she had been judging herself harshly for losing her yoga practice since her son had been born, that it seemed impossible to work

MAKING IT A BEYOND MOM BUSINESS • 179

full-time, be there for her family, and give herself as much time for yoga as she once had. But then she made a decision to lighten up her expectations on herself, at least for the time being. Maybe she wouldn't make her yoga class three times a week, but she could do one downward dog a day. That's right. In her home, even with her little one, she could find a downward dog every single day. Her body would lengthen, her breathing would deepen, her mind would settle. This she could manage every single day. She felt great about it and felt she was making contact with her yoga practice this way. And then the next revelation happened: downward dog would lead her into warrior two and peaceful warrior and so on and so forth. Before she knew it, she had her own little yoga practice going—sometimes for ten to fifteen minutes at a time. How good she felt about herself! Her mentality around her accomplishments had shifted and, therefore, she was able to find a new version of balance. By the time I saw her at our next retreat six months later, she was happy to report that as her son got bigger, she was able to make time for a weekly yoga class at a nearby studio but her lesson of "one downward dog a day" had stuck with all of us.

How can we make our own version of this story? Believe me, we all can. Whether it's a commitment to an outing with a girlfriend every two weeks, a massage every month, a workout twice a week, the non-mom parts of ourselves can still find space, we just need to adjust our expectations.

Admittedly, writing this book, growing the *Beyond Mom* site, planning events, being there for my two kids, my husband, my family and friends, is no easy feat. But with detailed calendar planning, the ability to say "no" when I must, and an adjustment to some of my expectations, all parts of my life have room to breathe. Are there sacrifices? Of course! But I feel balanced on most days. Here's a list of some of the things I've done to make it work, maybe these things will spark your own ideas and solution possibilities:

1. As a fitness enthusiast, I like to work out at least four days a week. For the few months that this book has been on deadline, I adjusted

my expectation to two. That hurts a little, but there are only so many hours in a day. What have I added? Stretching and toning exercises at home after the kids go to bed while I catch up on the news or have a phone chat with my best friend. It's only temporary, and I'm making it work. And if you'll notice, working out has not been totally cut out, its merely been adjusted.

2 I have a nanny for my little one and while my older one is in school full-time, his pick-up is still at three in the afternoon. I can't stop work at that time every day. So for a period of time, I've hired a part-time baby sitter to do his pick-up twice a week and hang out with him either out or at home until six in the evening. This buys me at least two more hours of work on those days. In turn, I've made the commitment to accompany him on Tuesdays to his basketball league—picking him up at school at three o'clock, having a snack together, and watching his basketball games with full attention from 4:15–5:30 p.m! He's thrilled to have my attention and to show me his basketball skills in real time. I try to find compromises within what can feel like a sacrifice. Similarly, I try to make it once a week to one of my baby's classes—her music class or her gym class. So I can be part of her growth and development in the outside world.

3 Healthy food is really important to me. I've stopped complaining about how much time it takes me to food shop and cook, and instead I build it in when I have the time. I've also started asking for help. Our wonderful nanny is happy to help me build my food creations so she has started helping me while the baby naps. This is a huge help but again, I spoke up for what I needed based on what's important to me.

4 I work ahead and stay highly organized, and I have discovered that most successful *Beyond Moms* do the same. Lists exist on our phones and on our counter top. Weekends are for online ordering of home supplies and Monday mornings are for food shopping (when the store is quieter and I can actually get it done more quickly). The house stays neat, which keeps my mind clear. I recently chatted to a friend who works long, demanding hours at Goldman Sachs and also manages her son and stepdaughter's busy schedules. "I stockpile birthday party gifts for the season to come," she explains. "I purchase some of the most popular gifts for kids my son's age at my local toy store. They wrap them nicely, I store them in my closet, and when a birthday party comes up, I know I'm prepared. No need to rush to the store during my few hours of free time." *Brilliant.* She also told me that she plans out her son's eating menu for the week while his nanny is in charge. This ensures that she knows what he's eating and she can make sure his food is ready and available. Her mind is more available for work and social activities when they arise. I love these concepts because they demonstrate how working ahead through excellent organization opens us up to so many more possibilities personally.

These are just a few examples of how I'm managing all the parts of my life that are important to me (and a few examples from my productive friends). Nothing feels like it's being disregarded, only re-adjusted and re-positioned so I can accomplish what I need to.

A *Beyond Mom* Company

I've often thought about a *Beyond Mom* company as an example of the fourth wave of feminism. We live in a time when a woman doesn't have to choose between her professional self and her mom self. She can create a fusion of experiences where cooking, baby classes, and workouts, are fit in between emails, networking events, and brainstorming. How we build that puzzle is our solution to discover. But the fact that we can do it is a beautiful thing.

Our experience as a mom who builds her dream is one to value and pursue, but what makes a *Beyond Mom* business unique?

A *Beyond Mom* business is fueled by the desire to solve a problem or pursue a deep passion—what else would be worth time away from our kids?

It has other women in mind. Most *Beyond Moms* want to connect, help, and be around other women in similar positions. Together we are stronger.

We are both devoted moms and fiercely clear that we are *more than moms*.

We understand that all parts of our lives must be acknowledged for our business life to thrive.

We understand that all parts of our lives must be acknowledged for our motherhood life to thrive.

We understand that we can't do it alone.

All moms experience guilt; this, I have sadly discovered, is a universal experience. Somehow, we believe there's something we're not doing well enough. Or should be doing much more of. I have realized though, that *Beyond Moms* have a bit less guilt because they actually do make time for all parts of their lives. Their jobs are to manage the frenetic energy of trying to wear a million hats every day. There's something about a *Beyond Mom* company that's incredibly heart-driven and honest. These companies stem from women who have done the rat race of corporate life and have chosen to create something on their own terms, with their own family in mind. With motherhood comes a sharpening of our intuition, an awareness of what works and doesn't, and a deep desire to make a difference in our own children's life . . . and often the lives of others too. Most will tell you that though we sacrifice sleep, our lives become a whole lot richer. That's what deep love will do. And from that deep love can come some of the most intriguing, beautiful, intelligent business ideas out there. Yes, great ideas don't just come from an idea that might make money (though that happens too). It comes from a source of love.

Becoming a mom is inherently a creation process. We build a baby in our womb and embark in the greatest work of our life. We are pushed to our very limits and discover our own capabilities in the process. It is said that the energy space where we carry our babies (the second chakra) is the same space where our ideas are born. How much sense this makes. A *Beyond Mom* business does not originate in our mind, it originates in our creation space, which is why these businesses are filled with so much love and goodwill.

And now, my dear friend, you must own all that you are capable of. You have birthed babies, you have the tools to get back to YOU, you have the tools to harness your idea and turn it in to a reality.

And, above all, sit with the greatest truth of all, the one that should empower you most:

You are a mom.

Now go *Beyond*.

Acknowledgments

I HONOR ALL THE *BEYOND MOMS* who have shared their stories, their support, their enthusiasm for my vision. Without you, none of this would be possible! A special thanks to the incredible contributors to this book and to my podcast—your insights based on your own expertise and winding journeys will make a real impact. You have inspired me and I know you will help all the women who read this book.

To my lifelong friends who have stood by me through thick and thin, you are my air! You have cheered me on, given me a break and a cocktail when I've needed one, and never stopped believing in me. To my newer mom friends, I cherish you! Tears, laughter, connection despite broken conversation—I value you beyond words!

For Jasmine Takanikos, who helped me conceive this brand years ago and who believed in this long before anyone even knew about it. For Nicola Kraus, writing coach and *Beyond Mom* extraordinaire, Lucinda Blumenfeld, amazing agent, mom, and advocate, Leah Zarra, most supportive editor out there, Ashley Bernardi, *Beyond Mom* public relations. For Aileen Haugh, who loves and supports my vision right along with me, Terri Hlavaty and my upstate team, thank you for your years of loyalty and love, Cornelia Innocent, caregiver full of heart—thank you for creating a foundation of support and motivation that has allowed me to step out into the world as my own version of *Beyond Mom.*

To the team of servers at Le Pain Quotidien Chelsea—as I wrote this book, you not only fed and caffeinated me, you encouraged me with your own creative stories and experiences. Each day, you infused your passions for your own projects and dreams into mine. You're all wonderful and you know who you are.

And thanks to all the mistakes, mess-ups, and failures. In the end, you were really none of those things, but were incredible learning lessons, beacons that shined light on the direction I really needed to go, and taught me the strength I never knew I had. For all of that, I'm grateful.

Even though I dedicated this book to my parents, my husband, and my kids, I feel I need to acknowledge them a little bit more.

Mom, you always said I was a writer. You were right. Thank you for loving me so deeply and for teaching me so much. I'll always be your sunshine girl.

Dad, you always said I was a writer and a business woman. You were also right. Your impact on me in the twenty-five years I had you was greater than many dads have in a lifetime. You are that energy, that inexplicable power that pushes me forward, even when I think I don't have it. Your spirit reminds me that I most certainly do. I feel you in my blood, in my thoughts, in everything I do. I will spend the rest of my life in your honor, making you proud. I love you, Beene.

Marquise, you walked in just when I ordered you. I was ready to be challenged, inspired, and loved, and you have done all that. I love raising a family with you. Thank you for believing in me so deeply and encouraging me every single day.

Micah, your powerful spirit has challenged me to grow—thanks for being the coolest kid on the block and for loving your mom so much. Without you, *Beyond Mom* wouldn't be! You fill me up. I hope this book makes you proud!

Zarah, having you as my daughter has been the greatest and most joyful surprise of my life! I plan to show you what it means to be a strong and loving woman, proud to be herself, committed to her mission and her family. Come with me on this ride.

I remember about three and a half months after my son was born, I finally asked my husband why he wasn't trying to have sex with me. He admitted that he was scared of hurting me and that kind of killed the vibe. I told him I wanted to try, even though I wasn't sure how it would feel. In the following week, when the moment didn't present itself, I felt my confidence and my mood plummeting—maybe he just wasn't into it. And then, out of the blue, one afternoon while our son napped, we found our moment. It was patient and slow and, for the most part, felt good. But the best part was that I felt connected to my husband again, on both a physical and emotional level. My state of mind immediately lifted. I was still *here*. *We* were still *here*. Don't underestimate the power of sexual connection, physically and emotionally, to bring us back to who we are.

Finding it difficult to find your mojo post-baby? Two simple *Beyond Mom* suggestions . . .

It's likely you and your partner haven't had a free moment to be adults together. Can you sneak away for one hour and have a glass of wine at local bar? If not, can you reserve that hour after baby goes to sleep to put on mellow music and talk about anything that is not parent-related? The point is that you have to find the ability to reconnect with the spark that brought you together originally. It's very difficult to find your mojo if you can't do this. As a *Beyond Mom* who just had her third child said to me recently, "We went out to dinner last night and I remembered, 'I *like* Matt!'" In the case of my husband and I, we've discovered that we don't need hours to reconnect (though it's nice when that happens). We often only need a short dinner or a walk in the neighborhood to feel that connection once again—it's about quality, not quantity. If you haven't found those moments, don't be surprised if it's difficult to get sexy.

Do you need some new undies? I say this half jokingly, but not really. I remember after my son was born, I was still wearing the giant grandma undies that fit diaper-sized pads. Oh yeah, and nursing bras. Hot. I remember the day I went and bought myself a pretty matching underwear and bra set when my son was only three months old. I hadn't lost the baby weight yet, and my breasts were clearly their